Becoming God-like
The Christian Path to Happiness

Becoming God-like
The Christian Path to Happiness

James Thomas Angelidis

Becoming God-like:
The Christian Path to Happiness

James Thomas Angelidis

www.jtangelidis.com

Copyright © 2023 by James Thomas Angelidis.

All rights reserved.

Cover Design:
Layout by James Thomas Angelidis.

Cover Image:
Iconography in Ascension Greek Orthodox Church in Fairview, NJ. Photograph by James Thomas Angelidis.

Author Image:
(On author bio page) Photograph taken of self by James Thomas Angelidis.

"every scribe who has been trained for the kingdom of heaven is like a householder who brings out of his treasure what is new and what is old."

- Jesus Christ (Matthew 13:52, RSV)

AUTHOR BIO

James Thomas Angelidis has been awarded three university degrees and has authored and independently published several Christian books. These accomplishments helped him become a Professor of Christian Theology at Seton Hall University in South Orange, New Jersey. Discover James's works on his website at www.jtangelidis.com.

DEDICATION

This book is dedicated to my sister Rosalyn's sons, my nephews Athan and Lucas. May you both always walk on the path to Salvation and strive for theosis. Know that light is good. It destroys darkness. It helps us see. Remember the power of light. Remember Jesus' proclamation in the Gospel According to John 8:12 (RSV) ... "I am the light of the world; he who follows me will not walk in darkness, but will have the light of life."

CONTENTS

PREFACE ... 17

1. PROLOGUE: HAPPINESS ... 21
   a. Author's Intention ... 21
   b. God and the Fallen World ... 24
   c. Youth and Maturity ... 25
   d. Misconception of Happiness ... 29
   e. Significance of Aristotle ... 31
   f. World Religions ... 35
   g. King of Kings ... 39
      i. Authority of Jesus ... 43
      ii. Authority of Jesus' Lessons ... 46
   h. Unclear Paths to Happiness ... 49
   i. Theosis ... 51

2. MONEY ... 53
   a. Lessons on Money from Jesus in the Gospels ... 53

           i. Primary Lessons on Money … 53
           ii. Supporting Lessons on Money … 64
        b. Lessons on Money from the Acts of the Apostles … 77
        c. Lessons on Money from the Letters … 78
        d. Lessons on Money from the Revelation to John … 84

  3. SEX … 85
        a. Lessons on Sex from Jesus in the Gospels … 85
           i. Primary Lessons on Sex … 85
           ii. Supporting Lessons on Sex … 95
        b. Lessons on Sex from the Acts of the Apostles … 101
        c. Lessons on Sex from the Letters … 101
        d. Lessons on Sex from the Revelation to John … 122

  4. POWER … 125
        a. Lessons on Power from Jesus in the Gospels … 125
           i. Primary Lessons on Power … 126

        ii. Supporting Lessons on Power ... 154
    b. Lessons on Power from the Acts of the Apostles ... 160
    c. Lessons on Power from the Letters ... 161
    d. Lessons on Power from the Revelation to John ... 168

5. FAME ... 169
    a. Lessons on Fame from Jesus in the Gospels ... 169
        i. Primary Lessons on Fame ... 169
        ii. Supporting Lessons on Fame ... 203
    b. Lessons on Fame from the Acts of the Apostles ... 211
    c. Lessons on Fame from the Letters ... 212
    d. Lessons on Fame from the Revelation to John ... 213

6. GREATNESS ... 215
    a. Lessons on Greatness from Jesus in the Gospels ... 216
        i. Primary Lessons on Greatness ... 216
        ii. Supporting Lessons on Greatness ... 249

    b. Lessons on Greatness from the Acts of the Apostles … 261
    c. Lessons on Greatness from the Letters … 262
    d. Lessons on Greatness from the Revelation to John … 262

7. EPILOGUE: THEOSIS … 263
    a. Introduction … 263
        i. Chapter Aim … 263
        ii. Defining Theosis … 265
        iii. Theosis Before Jesus Christ … 266
        iv. Theosis and Jesus Christ … 276
    b. Christian Doctrine of Theosis … 278
        i. In the New Testament … 279
        ii. After the New Testament … 285
    c. Role of God as Holy Trinity … 286
        i. God the Father … 288
        ii. God the Son … 290
        iii. God the Holy Spirit … 295
    d. Role of the Church Sacraments … 299
        i. Baptism … 300
        ii. The Eucharist … 301
    e. Role of the Human Being … 305
        i. Imitation of God … 308
        ii. Asceticism for God … 320

  iii. Contemplation of God … 325
 f. Experiencing Theosis … 333

BIBLIOGRAPHY … 345

==========================

PREFACE

==========================

I enjoy writing. For me, the process begins with reading and learning from books, and if inspired, I feel compelled to share what I have learned. I figure, if the material inspires me, it may inspire others, as well. I have the soul of a student and teacher, and few things bring me greater joy than sharing knowledge. And, the only knowledge that inspires me is that which helps me grow and become a better person. I primarily read nonfiction - specifically history, philosophy, religion, and theology. My personal library consists of about 900 books, which fill my apartment. I love books so much and have learned so much from them that I have written books. This is the eighth book that I have written, and all my books have to do with our Lord and Savior Jesus Christ.

After earning three university degrees - with awards, honors, and the highest grades - culminating in a Master of Arts degree in Christian Theology, I became a Professor of Christian Theology to undergraduate students at Seton Hall University in South Orange, NJ. I see myself in Jesus Christ's words when He said, "every scribe who has been trained for the kingdom of heaven is like a householder who brings out of his treasure what is new and what is old" (Matthew 13:52, RSV). With my background, I see myself as a scribe trained for the kingdom of heaven sharing treasure with my audience.

    This book began to take form during the 2022 summer on my author website at www.jtangelidis.com. I thought it would be a good way to attract readers to my work and show them the process of how a book is formed. They would be able to follow my work in progress with each post. The topic for my new book would have to do with the pursuit of happiness as taught by the Christian Faith.

    Like everyone, I want to be happy, and as a reader, academic and scholar, I knew I would find answers for the topic in books. I was most interested in understanding happiness as taught by Jesus who is my Lord, Savior, and God. However, I believe that even if Jesus is not a person's Lord, Savior and God, His teachings could still be intriguing to a person by virtue of Jesus' extraordinary impact on humankind's history in the world. It is impossible to deny Jesus' influence, even if you see Him as simply an extraordinary human being.

    So, on my website, on a webpage titled "Forthcoming," I provided free Christian Bible lessons for my new book. One by one, I posted my work from my investigation into the most popular paths to happiness - money, sex, power, fame, greatness - as taught by Jesus and the New Testament. Every couple of weeks, I posted on my website a document with a comprehensive collection of lessons on each path. Ever wonder what Jesus taught about money, sex, power, or fame? What did Jesus teach regarding greatness? With the posts on my website, I made it easy to find out. I advertised each document on social media, advertised my other books, and then I repeated the process with all five paths. I posted my comprehensive collections together as the "Popular Paths to Happiness: Lessons from Jesus and the New Testament."

Money, sex, power, fame, and greatness are mighty worldly forces. They are humankind's foremost motivators, influences, and stimulants. They are also the most popular paths to happiness. In each of my documents, I cited passages with primary lessons and supporting lessons on each topic by Jesus Christ in the Gospels as well as additional lessons from the remaining New Testament. I believe my website documents were what the United States media calls PSAs (Public Service Announcements) for the benefit of my audience. I was trying to get people to read the Bible, so I was happy to share my collection of Christian Bible lessons for free on my website. Now, in this book, you will find the lessons I initially provided on my website about the popular paths to happiness as taught by Jesus and the New Testament.

In this book on happiness, I also include Christian lessons from the Church's greatest Saints and Theologians on the Christian view of living your best life known as the blessing of theosis, which is when a person becomes a god - through likeness to and union with God - attaining one's fullest divine potential. The Orthodox Church emphasizes that theosis is the purpose and goal of life. Theosis is the Church's prescribed path to happiness in this life, in the afterlife, and in the General Resurrection. The doctrine of theosis is the cherished theological gem of the Orthodox Church.

As a student, I did the homework, and as a teacher, I shared my knowledge. This work was for my benefit as well as the benefit of my audience. This book is unique. The approach of identifying and elaborating on the popular paths to happiness with Christian Bible lessons has never been done before. I have never come across a book like the one you are reading. The result of my labor is this book - *Becoming God-like: The Christian Path to Happiness* - and I pray it does much good for God.

Read, learn, and enjoy.

With agape love in Christ Jesus,
James Thomas Angelidis

(1)

PROLOGUE

HAPPINESS

(a) <u>Author's Intention</u>

Compared to other faiths, philosophies and lifestyles, Christianity has a unique view of life in the world and has its own approach to living. As a result, Christianity has a distinctive understanding regarding happiness. It may seem strange that a religion that is based on love (agape love) does not guarantee constant happiness for its believers in this life. However, as we all know, life is not easy and is often a struggle - and this reality of life is no different for the faithful Christian. All faiths, philosophies, and lifestyles have an approach on how to attain happiness. I believe that is one major reason people go to religion - to ease suffering and find happiness, which are common goals for all human beings. No one wants to suffer, and everyone wants to be happy.

Happiness is the human person's most desirable and seemingly elusive goal. There are several paths to the goal of happiness, and the most prominent paths are the inspiration for the chapter topics in this book. This work is an investigation and education on the quest for happiness in this life for the faithful Christian. I write to share with others what helps me in this journey of life, and, perhaps, others can benefit, as well, from what I have discovered and put in writing. I have learned from the world's greatest scholars, philosophers, theologians, and Saints, as well as from God Himself.

This book is a guide and reference manual on how a Christian can live his or her best life. It will lead you away from the pitfalls of suffering that trap many people in this world, and it will direct you on the correct path to happiness. This book is an investigation into the Christian understanding of living happy. There is more to it than you may think, and you may be surprised at what you learn. We people may have different interests, but we all are common in nature as human beings. This book will cover much of our human experience. You will find answers in this work as you read. How much a person learns will depend on how much a person already knows, but I do believe this work has something to offer all readers and is worth reading. There is treasure in this work.

The reader may be wondering what type of literature is *Becoming God-like: The Christian Path to Happiness*? It is not strictly academic, but I do hope to educate. I will reference important passages from the Christian Scriptures. I will not be inventing anything. This work will not result in revolutionary conclusions. It is a study. However, there will be useful and enlightening resolutions with insights and answers on how a faithful Christian can find happiness in this life before Eternity. If a Christian is blessed in Eternity, he or she will experience uninterrupted eternal happiness, light, and love. This book will direct the reader to a blessed eternal life, but from its conception, it has been about living a blessed life in this world. The word philosophy comes from the Greek language and translates into English as "love of wisdom." There is wisdom in this book. However, this book is predominantly theology, which is a word that has Greek origins, too, and translates into English as "the discourse or reasoning of God." God is fundamental to a Christian's happiness in this life and in the afterlife. This book will focus on the human being in the world with God as the Source of light, love, and life. This work is a culmination of over twenty years of reading, studying, and writing as a Christian.

(b) God and the Fallen World

God wants us to be happy because he loves us - which has been made clear to the world by the birth, life, teachings, death, Resurrection, and Ascension of our Lord and Savior Jesus Christ. As John 3:16 (RSV) illustrates,

> For God so loved the world that he gave his only Son, that whoever believes in him should not perish but have eternal life.

God loves us and only wants good for us. However, the world has fallen from its intended state of purity as a paradise because of the evil one, the adversary, the devil, Satan. The world is fallen, dark, chaotic, corrupt, and confused because of the evil one's influence. In the world, there is good as well as evil, just as there is light as well as darkness. Our forebears Adam and Eve were tempted by the evil one, and because of the evil one's influence, they disobeyed God's commands. Because of our forebears, we inherit the trials of life. We repeat the sins we have learned from previous generations. However, we can be saved from this world's madness by abiding by and abiding in our Lord and Savior Jesus Christ. He helps us return to God the Father and Paradise in Eternity. The world is indeed fallen (already, in the second generation of humanity, Cain murders his brother Abel), but it is not lost because Jesus has given us the way to Salvation. If we follow Jesus, we can be saved and enjoy some happiness in this life that will lead us to eternal life where happiness is perfect, uninterrupted, and everlasting. With the help of Jesus, we can travel on the path to happiness in this life.

In addition, blessings from God are necessary for happiness, but God's blessings do not equate to uninterrupted happiness for us in this fallen world. This is not God's fault and is rather our fault. God continuously blesses those who are devoted to Him, but we do not always see it - which illustrates the relationship between Perfect God and imperfect human beings.

(c) **Youth and Maturity**

As we age and grow, our approaches to happiness usually shift. When we are young, most of us search for excitement and adventure. We seek out the thrills in life assuming they are the greatest moments of life. We often dare death to prove to ourselves that we are alive. Many people jump out of airplanes for pleasure to attain a spirited feeling. As youth, we want excitement and adventure, which often leads to carelessness and recklessness.

Unlike the young, the mature want peace. This may sound dull to the young, but the mature know the beauty and joy of peace. All the world religions prescribe methods to attain peace for their devotees. In Greek Orthodox Christianity, the stillness, silence, rest, quiet within the soul is called "hesychia." Men and women of all walks of life - though predominantly monastics - are encouraged to attain, cultivate, and maintain hesychia for the benefit of their souls. Hesychia is key to happiness and is a fruit of theosis. The Epilogue of this book is on theosis - the condition that will lead to hesychia. For now, it is important to note that the mature know the value of inward stillness, silence, rest, quiet and consider it one of the highest goods in human life. There is a reason the letters R.I.P. are associated with tombstones. R.I.P. stands for Rest In Peace. It is a simple prayer to God for the departed human being which recognizes and acknowledges the turbulence of life and which expresses the hope that the departed is now resting easy in peace with God.

When a person does not grow gracefully, the mentality of youthfulness and the mentality of maturity conflict. A struggle arises within the person's soul. There is that image of the devil on one shoulder and an angel on the other shoulder each whispering in one ear of a person in conflict. Who should a person listen to - the devil or the angel? Should we do the bad act or the good act? The person has reached a fork with two paths on the road of life. The older the person, the more serious the consequences of an action for worse or better.

The hope is that the youth will never fall victim to the carelessness and recklessness that tempt them in life. It is the responsibility of those who are older to guide the young, especially the youngest. The older an individual is, the more responsible the individual will be for his or her own actions. If the young do fall victim to carelessness and recklessness, the prayer is that they recover and grow to develop mature and wise minds and choose to serve God. The hope is that they realize hesychia's benefits and choose to cultivate hesychia within their souls.

Another part of life that the youth and mature do not see in the same way is health. Good health is a virtue and a blessing. It is something desirable and at the same time, it is beneficial. There is bodily health, mental health, and spiritual health. Instinctively, we all want to be healthy in body, mind, and spirit. This book is fundamentally about the mind and spirit, but for the moment, I would like to focus on bodily health.

When I was a child, my grandparents and older aunts and older uncles would often speak about the value of good health. It was common talk. I remember hearing often from them about the benefits and importance of good health. Those sentiments became trite and cliché in my mind, and as I grew, the sentiment lacked potency. However, as I matured and increased in age, I understood the relevance and truth of my elders' words. That older generation spoke about health often because it was a solid truth for them that I eventually understood, as well, when I matured with wisdom. For example, if you cannot walk, you cannot enjoy an evening stroll in the neighborhood. If you are deaf, you cannot enjoy music. If you are a diabetic with high blood sugar, you are limited to the choices of sweets for dessert. Lack of health and downright sickness prevent the full enjoyment of life. Good health does not guarantee happiness, but good health makes one more likely to enjoy happiness. Without good health, one is less likely to enjoy happiness.

Health is good because it fosters life. Sickness is bad because it can lead to death. More important than good physical health is a healthy soul, which stems from a good character and a virtuous life with Jesus Christ. Good physical health with a good soul will lead to happiness, and bad physical health with a good soul can also lead to happiness. However, good physical health with a sick soul will never lead to happiness, and bad physical health with a sick soul leads to death and hell.

The hope is that with maturity comes wisdom. However, the devil has a way interfering with a mature person's walk on the path to wisdom and happiness. The devil often leads a mature person down a path that is a misconception of happiness.

(d) **Misconception of Happiness**

Everyone wants to be happy, and we all have an idea of what happiness looks like. I remember when I was a child, I had an idea of what happiness would look like as an adult. I believe this idea is shared with others and is a collective general consensus of what happiness looks like. I believe, as human beings, we share a common idea about happiness, but this idea is a misconception of reality. This common shared belief is actually inaccurate and not true. I believe this idea has been around ever since people began living together in societies and began laboring with one another. This idea is shared by most people, but in the past, it has been lived out by only the most financially wealthy. Today, in the United States of America, I believe more people have this dream and could potentially live it out, but it is still a misconception of happiness. People work at their jobs and make money for the future with the dream of retirement. What does this retirement look like? Most people have not thought deeply about it, but they know that it is good, that it is a goal, and that it is desirable. In fact, people work harder and harder to collect more and more money, so they can retire earlier in life - that is how powerful the dream is. People of every economic class have a similar dream, perhaps not exactly the same dream, but definitely a similar idea.

Generally, in this dream, people picture themselves as Roman Caesars who are fed grapes fresh from their personal vineyards and who drink wine that flows endlessly. At any moment during the day, they can feast on and indulge in the finest foods. In this dream, the greatest luxury that people expect to enjoy is free time to do all the pleasurable activities that they enjoy. However, for most people, the dream of retirement and reality of retirement are not the same. Enjoyable activities are only enjoyable for a limited time. At some point, pleasure will become mundane, as well. We all know this to some degree, yet we have this dream, nonetheless. It is also worthy to note that this dream stems from the image of Roman Caesars who surely indulged in these comforts, but, ironically, were often murdered by their enemies or even those they considered friends. Not even Roman Caesars lived out the dream, yet the image remains.

There is another dream that is related and also pervades the human mind. And, that is the endless vacation. With sun, beaches and leisure, people dream of living what seems like an easy life.

However, this, too, is only enjoyable until it becomes mundane. It is superficial and lacks nourishment that would satisfy the soul (and a healthy soul is the key to happiness). If this was your dream, you may be sad to hear that the human spirit will never be fulfilled by this perpetual leisure.

I, too, had dreams like these, but I questioned them with serious thought, did some reading, and observed people in the world to realize they are inaccurate portrayals of reality. This may sound disappointing, but do not distress; there is a way of living that will generate a happier life because it is real and true. Anything that is real and true will always be better than something that is fake and false because it is honest and will not deceive you. Reality, Truth, and Honesty are attributes of God. Fakeness, falsehood, and deception are works of the devil. We will explore authentic ways of living in this work.

(e) **Significance of Aristotle**

Aristotle was an Ancient Greek Philosopher who died in 322 BC. He is a part of a wonderful educational lineage and tradition that emerged in Ancient Greece. This educational lineage and tradition began with the Pre-Socratic philosophers, and grew with Socrates, Plato, and Aristotle. A student of Aristotle, Alexander the Great promoted the ideas of Ancient Greece, and through his conquests, Hellenism (Greek culture) permeated the world. Hellenism has influenced the world for over the past 2,000 years and continues to do so today.

Because of Aristotle's prominence, authority, and influence in the philosophical enterprise, Catholic Saint and Doctor of the Church Thomas Aquinas, in his masterpiece *Summa Theologica*, refers to Aristotle as simply "the Philosopher." The simple designation "the Philosopher" honors Aristotle and shows how important he was and is in the landscape of Western Thought.

Aristotle is so important to Western Thought that in E. H. Gombrich's classic for young adults - *A Little History of the World* - the author explains that Aristotle was "the teacher of mankind for 2,000 years… In the 2,000 years that followed, whenever people failed to agree on one thing or another, they turned to his writings. He was their referee. What Aristotle said must be right. For what he had done was to gather together all the knowledge of his time. He wrote about the natural sciences - the stars, animals and plants; about history and people living together in a state - what we call politics; about the right way to reason - logic; and the right way to behave - ethics. He wrote about poetry and its beauty. And last of all he wrote down his own thoughts on a god who hovered impassive and unseen above the vault of heaven" (Gombrich, 64).

I believe Gombrich wrote a beautiful epitaph to honor Aristotle for the youth, so the youth would know how important Aristotle is. Not even Socrates or Plato is given such praise in Gombrich's book. Of the Ancient Greek Philosophers, Plato is dearest to my heart. As a university student, I was most mesmerized with Plato, but as I have grown, I have learned to respect the greatness of Aristotle. The two philosophers and educators had different styles of thought and writing, but both men, along with Socrates, were virtuous wise men blessed by God.

For this introduction, I single out Aristotle from all the other deep and insightful Ancient Greek Philosophers because of his investigation into happiness, which he examines at length in his book - *Nicomachean Ethics*. The title is a reference to either Aristotle's son or father, both named Nicomachus. It is the preeminent work on ethics by the famous philosopher and educator. It is practical philosophy about how men can live best, including how to live a happy life.

Aristotle provides a formal definition for happiness. He explains that "the good of man, happiness, is some kind of activity of the soul in conformity with virtue" (*Nicomachean Ethics*, 1.9). Happiness is an activity. It is something we have to work at attaining, sustaining, and maintaining. Aristotle's philosophy is unlike the "Misconception of

Happiness" dream that I elaborated on earlier in this Prologue. The misconception of happiness dream is neither an activity of the soul (it's not even an activity) nor is it in conformity with virtue. This realization may be startling, but it is true. The misconception of happiness dream is a seductive lie. Nonetheless, happiness is attainable, and by the end of this book, you will learn about the Christian path to happiness, which is in agreement with Aristotle's definition of happiness.

    Aristotle was a powerful influence on me when I conceived this book. In *Nicomachean Ethics*, Aristotle ponders and examines the various views on the highest good, namely, happiness. He explains that men have different views on happiness - the highest good - according to the lives they lead. Some men believe happiness comes from **pleasure**; others believe it is from **honor**; still others believe it is from **excellence**; while others believe it is from **wealth**; and yet others believe it is from **contemplative life** (*Nicomachean Ethics*, 1.5). With these classifications by Aristotle, I believe my audience can see from where and how I derived the popular paths to happiness - money, sex, power, fame, greatness - that I examine in this book; although, I use terminology more closely used by Jesus and the New Testament writers. Aristotle was a major stimulus for this book, and he inspired me to seek answers to what my Lord and Savior Jesus Christ says about these popular paths to happiness.

(f) **World Religions**

What do the World Religions teach about God? All six major World Religions (Hinduism, Taoism, Buddhism, Judaism, Christianity, Islam) confess that there is a Supreme Source of authentic pure life that is connected to each and every human being. Truths about the Supreme Source can be found in all the World Religions. All the World Religions teach that the purpose of human existence and the goal of human life is union with the Supreme Source - the Supreme Reality, Truth, Power, Existence, Essence, Spirit, Soul, Being - who many people call God. The Supreme Source is the Source of all that is good and possesses only positive attributes and no negative attributes. Therefore, union with the Supreme Source will benefit us and make us happier people. This theology is the greatest universal belief among the World Religions, and it is one major reason people go to religion. All the World Religions teach a similar idea.

The religions of the East are good. They are philosophical and have come to know God through human inquiry. They teach some truths, but not the complete truth. They, too, have answers and understand that there is a Supreme Source of authentic pure life, but they do not recognize or know this Source as the One Almighty God. Hindus refer to the Soul of the Cosmos as Brahman. Taoists refer to the Source of Heaven and Earth and the Way It operates as the Tao. Buddhists believe in ultimate universal Truths and ultimate Law, which they call the Dharma. What the three Eastern World Religions teach about God's Power is true, but they do not recognize the Source of power and life as God.

From the Western World - Jews, Christians, and Muslims all believe in the One Almighty God. Jews believe He is so Holy that a person must not dare say or write His Name. Christians call Him Heavenly Father. Muslims say He is the Beneficent, the Merciful. The three Western Religions are monotheistic and agree that there is One Almighty God, but Jews and Muslims do not recognize the Divinity of Jesus as Christians do.

Jews and Muslims overlook the truth that Jesus is the Christ and God Incarnate because they have not thoroughly examined the Jewish Scriptures, or if they have examined the Jewish Scriptures, it is because of the hardness of their hearts.

Jesus fulfills the Jewish Old Testament prophecy of the Christ (the Messiah). For powerful confirmation, please read "The Servant, a Light to the Nations" in Isaiah 42:1-9 and "The Suffering Servant" in Isaiah 52:13-53:12.

Jesus also fulfills the Jewish Old Testament prophecy of God Incarnate. For powerful confirmation, please read "The Righteous Reign of the Coming King" in Isaiah 9:1-7, particularly verse 6.

In Matthew 10:40-42 (RSV), Jesus explains,

> 40 "He who receives you receives me, and he who receives me receives him who sent me. 41 He who receives a prophet because he is a prophet shall receive a prophet's reward, and he who receives a righteous man because he is a righteous man shall receive a righteous man's reward. 42 And whoever gives to one of these little ones even a cup of cold water because he is a disciple, truly, I say to you, he shall not lose his reward."

Some Jews may say Jesus was a righteous man, and Muslims believe Jesus was a mighty prophet, but neither would confess, as Christians do, that Jesus is the Divine Son of Almighty God and that He is the embodiment of Almighty God. All who believe in the Divinity of Jesus and live according to Jesus' teachings, as revealed in the New Testament Gospels, will be given the right to enter Paradise because they acknowledge Him as the Way, and the Truth, and the Life (John 14:6). He is the Door of the Sheepfold and all who enter through Him will enter Paradise (John 10:1-21).

As I mentioned, the World Religions teach and share valuable truths. There is Christian encouragement for this point of view. On my website's webpage "Apologetics," I note that:

> In the 20th century, the Catholic Church spoke about a theology called "Hierarchy of Truths" to initiate Christian ecumenism and interfaith dialogue. The Hierarchy of Truths Theology is very real and applicable to Christianity, religion, philosophy and humanity.
>
> (Angelidis, "In the Spirit of Truth: Identifying My Three Theological Treatises in Church Tradition," 2017; 2019. https://www.jtangelidis.com/apologetics.html. Accessed 5-10-2023.)

A universal truth among all the World Religions is that a person will benefit by uniting with the Supreme Source of all that is good. And, for Christians, the Supreme Source of all that is good is God, and He is our Heavenly Father.

We all have an idea of what a good father is like. Some of us have had good fathers in our lives, some of us have not, but for Christians, God is the Perfect Heavenly Father Who participates in our lives. It is beautiful because it implies an intimate personal relationship with God that is filled with love - a divine heavenly love. And, we know God as

Father because of Jesus who teaches us about God the Father. We are able to develop a relationship with God the Father and attain union with Him through His Son - Jesus the Christ. Christianity believes that Jesus the Christ is the Way to God the Father. Christianity teaches that only through Jesus the Christ can one make it to God the Father. And, this is the path we will continue to follow in this book. The Christian path to God.

(g) King of Kings

The most inspiring person in world history is Jesus - the King of kings. There is a powerful and moving sermon on the life of Jesus Christ that illustrates His position as the King of kings. It is from a sermon that is attributed to Pastor Dr. James Allan Francis who died in 1928. And, it is known as - One Solitary Life. It is a bit famous. It explains,

> Here is a man who was born in an obscure village, the child of a peasant woman. He grew up in another obscure village, where He worked in a carpenter shop until He was thirty, and then for three years He was an itinerant preacher.

He never wrote a book. He never held an office. He never owned a home. He never had a family. He never went to college. He never put his foot inside a big city. He never traveled two hundred miles from the place where He was born. He never did one of the things that usually accompany greatness. He had no credentials but Himself. He had nothing to do with this world except the naked power of His divine manhood.

While still a young man, the tide of public opinion turned against Him. His friends ran away. One of them denied Him. He was turned over to His enemies. He went through the mockery of a trial. He was nailed to a cross between two thieves. His executioners gambled for the only piece of property He had on earth while He was dying—and that was his coat. When he was dead, He was taken down and laid in a borrowed grave through the pity of a friend.

Nineteen wide centuries have come and gone and today He is the centerpiece of the human race and the leader of the column of progress. I am far within the mark when I say that all the armies that ever marched, and all the navies that ever were built, and all the parliaments that ever sat, all the kings that ever reigned, put together have not affected the life of man upon this earth as powerfully as has that One Solitary Life.

(https://www.bartleby.com/73/916.html. Accessed 1-27-2022. Paragraph separation added by James Thomas Angelidis.)

This little piece was popular with American politicians and celebrities in the 1970s and 1980s during the Christmas season. And, it often appeared on holiday greeting cards. In New York City at Radio City Music Hall, this passage appears during the annual "Christmas Spectacular." The sermon is not perfect. There are a couple of inaccuracies, even so the message remains intact (It states, "He never put his foot inside a big city" - which is inaccurate because Jesus visited the city of Jerusalem more than once and Jerusalem was a major city; although, it was not as big as today's cities. It also states, "He never did one of the things that usually accompany greatness" - that depends on how one defines greatness because the faithful believe in His miracles, love, and teachings. However, it appears the author means how one becomes great in a conventional sense.).

This piece describes the human being type facts of Jesus, but then the astonishing and extraordinary repercussions of that Single Life. The underlying message of the sermon is that there is more to Jesus than the bare facts of His life, as made clear by what has happened to the world because of that One Solitary Life. It is a powerful message for both believers and unbelievers, alike.

Let us take this idea of One Solitary Life one step further. I would like to point out to you an obvious, but profound observation about Jesus' impact on the world. Over 2,000 years since His advent, Jesus is everywhere. All over the world, architects build churches for Him, painters imagine His likeness, sculptures chisel His image, poets honor Him, and musicians create songs for Him. Martyrs have died for Him, and Saints have lived for Him. Every human being in modern civilization has heard of Jesus and has a view or opinion of Him. Each religion has a different belief about Him, but there can be no doubt about the magnitude of His influence. No one on this planet can deny how enormous Jesus is. No human being to ever walk this earth has had a greater impact on human culture and history. No one else compares. For example, our concept of time hinges on His birth.

Let us reflect on the letters BC. What does BC stand for? BC = Before Christ. Let us reflect on the letters AD. What does AD stand for? AD = Anno Domini, which is Latin for "In the year of our Lord" - beginning with the birth of our Lord.

Jesus is the Lord. This is all because of one Man. The year AD 2023 has meaning because of this one Man's existence. Most of the world and its understanding of time year by year has adapted itself around the birth of One Individual whose name is Jesus - an Individual who lived over 2,000 years ago. Most people who live their lives in this world are never remembered, but Jesus is not only remembered, He is revered and worshiped. That is quite an impressive thought whether or not you are a Christian.

To many of you, this insight or observation is not something new, but it is, nonetheless, an insight that is profound. Regardless of one's faith, there is a legitimate claim here to call Jesus the "King of kings" and "God." He is the Greatest. And, this is because His presence and power live in our world in a very supernatural, mystical, and divine sense that can be mystifying to a non-believer, but for the faithful Christian, they are realer than life itself. I know Jesus to be the Way, the Truth, and the Life because of the Old Testament prophecies He fulfilled, His workings in the world, and what is confirmed in my soul from His love and His teachings. We Christians know Jesus as the King of kings who will forever sit on His eternal righteous throne exalted in glory surrounded by the Holy Angels and Saints who we hope to join in everlasting light, love, and happiness.

(i) Authority of Jesus

In the Gospel According to John, there are seven well-known "I am" statements by Jesus that are strong examples depicting His authority as the King of kings and which I find particularly inspiring. Below are the seven statements, which are powerful and illuminating.

> In John 6:35 (RSV), Jesus proclaims, "I am the bread of life; he who comes to me shall not hunger, and he who believes in me shall never thirst."

> In John 8:12 (RSV), Jesus proclaims, "I am the light of the world; he who follows me will not walk in darkness, but will have the light of life."

> In John 10:7-9 (RSV), Jesus proclaims, "Truly, truly, I say to you, I am the door of the sheep... if any one enters by me, he will be saved, and will go in and out and find pasture."

> In John 10:11 (RSV), Jesus proclaims, "I am the good shepherd. The good shepherd lays down his life for the sheep."

In John 11:25-26 (RSV), Jesus proclaims, "I am the resurrection and the life;[a] he who believes in me, though he die, yet shall he live, 26 and whoever lives and believes in me shall never die."

In John 14:6 (RSV), Jesus proclaims, "I am the way, and the truth, and the life; no one comes to the Father, but by me."

In John 15:1-11 (RSV), Jesus proclaims, "I am the true vine, and my Father is the vinedresser. 2 Every branch of mine that bears no fruit, he takes away, and every branch that does bear fruit he prunes, that it may bear more fruit. 3 You are already made clean by the word which I have spoken to you. 4 Abide in me, and I in you. As the branch cannot bear fruit by itself, unless it abides in the vine, neither can you, unless you abide in me. 5 I am the vine, you are the branches. He who abides in me, and I in him, he it is that bears much fruit, for apart from me you can do nothing. 6 If a man does not abide in me, he is cast forth as a branch and withers; and the branches are gathered, thrown into the fire and burned. 7 If you abide in me, and my words abide in you, ask whatever you will, and it shall be done for you. 8 By this my Father is glorified, that you bear much fruit, and so prove to be my disciples. 9 As the Father has loved me, so have I loved you; abide in my love. 10 If you keep my commandments, you will abide in my love, just as I have kept my Father's commandments and abide in his love. 11 These things I have spoken to you, that my joy may be in you, and that your joy may be full."

Jesus proclaims an additional "I am" statement in the Gospel According to John that is even more authoritative, powerful, and extraordinary than the well-known statements cited above. In John 8:58 (RSV), Jesus proclaims, "Truly, truly, I say to you, before Abraham was, I am." With this statement, Jesus declares He is God. This proclamation is further explained in the last chapter of this book in the section "God the Son" (7.c.ii).

(ii) Authority of Jesus' Lessons

As the King of kings, Jesus spoke with authority. Below are five passages from the Gospels that are strong examples depicting the authority of Jesus' lessons and which I find particularly inspiring.

In Matthew 7:13-14 (RSV), Jesus teaches about The Narrow Gate… "Enter by the narrow gate; for the gate is wide and the way is easy,[a] that leads to destruction, and those who enter by it are many. 14 For the gate is narrow and the way is hard, that leads to life, and those who find it are few."

In Matthew 7:24-29 (RSV) (Luke 6), Jesus teaches about Hearers and Doers… "Every one then who hears these words of mine and does them will be like a wise man who built his house upon the rock; 25 and the rain fell, and the floods came, and the winds blew and beat upon that house, but it did not fall, because it had been founded on the rock. 26 And every one who hears these words of mine and does not do them will be like a foolish man who built his house upon the sand; 27 and the rain fell, and the floods came, and the winds blew and beat against that house, and it fell; and great was the fall of it." 28 And when Jesus finished these sayings, the crowds were astonished at his teaching, 29 for he taught them as one who had authority, and not as their scribes."

In Matthew 24:32-35 (RSV) (Mark 13, Luke 21), Jesus teaches The Lesson of the Fig Tree… "From the fig tree learn its lesson: as soon as its branch becomes tender and puts forth its leaves, you know that summer is near. 33 So also, when you see all these things, you know that he is near, at the very gates. 34 Truly, I say to you, this generation will not pass away till all these things take place. 35 Heaven and earth will pass away, but my words will not pass away."

In Luke 10:38-42 (RSV), we learn Jesus Visits Martha and Mary… "Now as they went on their way, he entered a village; and a woman named Martha received him into her house. 39 And she had a sister called Mary, who sat at the Lord's feet and listened to his teaching. 40 But Martha was distracted with much serving; and she went to him and said, "Lord, do you not care that my sister has left me to serve alone? Tell her then to help me." 41 But the Lord answered her, "Martha, Martha, you are anxious and troubled about many things; 42 one thing is needful.[e] Mary has chosen the good portion, which shall not be taken away from her."

In John 8:31-32 (RSV), Jesus teaches about True Disciples… "If you continue in my word, you are truly my disciples, 32 and you will know the truth, and the truth will make you free."

(h) Unclear Paths to Happiness

In Christianity, we know God exists, and just as real as God, so is the devil. We know the devil as the evil one, the adversary, the enemy, and Satan. The Old Testament talks about the devil, and so do Jesus and the writers of the New Testament. The devil is seductive. He knows he has power over people, and he uses this power to influence people all the time. He is relentless and does not stop. He is the deceiver and is selfish and only cares about himself. As Scripture declares, "woe to you, O earth and sea, for the devil has come down to you in great wrath, because he knows that his time is short!" (Revelation 12:12b, RSV). He wants as many people as possible to join him in the Pit of Hell. Every temptation that he uses is for his own selfish benefit. He does not care about our wellbeing. He does not want what is good for us. And, for this reason alone, we should not listen to him. Never - regardless of who the person is - listen to a person, if that person does not have your best interest in mind. The devil is the worst and does not care about us, so we must not listen to him or be influenced by his temptations.

There are a few mighty worldly forces the devil uses to seduce us and lead us away from God and into the Pit of Hell. After God, the most powerful influences, motivators, and stimulants on people in the world are money, sex, power, fame, and greatness. As I mentioned earlier, I derived these influences - these paths - from Aristotle's *Nicomachean Ethics* (1.5) where he talks about pleasure, honor, excellence, and wealth. These popular paths to happiness are not necessarily bad, but they are not necessarily good, either. They are ambiguous and unclear. These paths often lead people astray on the way to God. These paths are bad when a person does not have God as his goal, but with God, they can lead to good results. In this book, you will learn about these popular paths to happiness according to the teachings of Jesus Christ and the New Testament. You will learn what the Good Lord and the New Testament writers advise when approaching these popular paths to happiness.

I have never seen these paths illuminated before with the teachings of Jesus Christ and the New Testament, nor have I ever seen the New Testament material presented in this way. This study and approach are unique. When I was young, learning and growing, I searched for material like this and never found it, but it has always been on my mind. I remember thinking about how convenient and helpful it would be if I had a comprehensive collection of all of Jesus' lessons on money. This way, I would have a complete and full understanding of what the Lord wants us to know. This book that you are reading is something I was in search of for myself. And, by not finding anything of the sort, I decided to do the homework for myself. Now that this material is published, my audience can learn from and benefit from my homework, as well.

For people who are wondering, the lessons are quoted from the Revised Standard Version (RSV) of the Bible. The lessons in each section are predominately in the order they appear in the New Testament. I have kept the lessons pure without much commentary, so they can speak for themselves.

(i) **Theosis**

Money, sex, power, fame, and greatness are the most popular paths to happiness. Jesus and the New Testament teach unique lessons about these paths. In this book, you will find a comprehensive collection of lessons from Jesus and the New Testament on money, sex, power, fame, and greatness. And, if you follow Jesus and apply His lessons to your life, you can attain the fullest measure of happiness possible in this world with the blessing of theosis, which is when a person becomes a god -

through likeness to and union with God - attaining one's fullest divine potential. Biology teaches us that we are animals, but God reassures us that we can become divine. Theosis is the Christian path to happiness. In this book, you will learn about theosis and how to become God-like.

In this book's Epilogue, I will highlight the nature, framework, and elements of theosis. Consider this chapter as the formula for theosis, and if you apply this chapter (and book) to yourself and make it a part of your lifestyle, you will be on the path to theosis and attain all the good qualities that come with it - including peace and happiness - to the fullest measure a person can in this world. We know this to be true from the teachings of Jesus and the testimonies of the Church's greatest Saints and Theologians.

(2)

MONEY

This chapter contains a comprehensive collection of lessons on money from Jesus and the New Testament.

It is worth noting that the three Synoptic Gospels (Matthew, Mark, Luke) talk a lot about money and that the Gospel According to John does not talk directly about money.

(a) <u>Lessons on Money from Jesus in the Gospels: 24 Passages</u>

(i) Primary Lessons on Money: 12 Passages

1.
=====

In Matthew 6, Jesus teaches "Concerning Treasures."

19 "Do not lay up for yourselves treasures on earth, where moth and rust[c] consume and where thieves break in and steal, 20 but lay up for yourselves treasures in heaven, where neither moth nor rust[d] consumes and where thieves do not break in and steal. 21 For where your treasure is, there will your heart be also.

2.
=====

In Matthew 6, Jesus teaches about "Serving Two Masters."

24 "No one can serve two masters; for either he will hate the one and love the other, or he will be devoted to the one and despise the other. You cannot serve God and mammon [Mammon is a Semitic word for money or riches].

3.
=====

In Matthew 6 (Luke 12), Jesus teaches "Do Not Worry."

25 "Therefore I tell you, do not be anxious about your life, what you shall eat or what you shall drink, nor about your body, what you shall put on. Is not life more than food, and the body more than clothing? 26 Look at the birds of the air: they neither sow nor reap nor gather into barns, and yet your heavenly Father feeds them. Are you not of more value than they? 27 And which of you by being anxious can add one cubit to his span of life?[f] 28 And why are you anxious about clothing? Consider the lilies of the field, how they grow; they neither toil nor spin; 29 yet I tell you, even Solomon in all his glory was not arrayed like one of these. 30 But if God so clothes the grass of the field, which today is alive and tomorrow is thrown into the oven, will he not much more clothe you, O men of little faith? 31 Therefore do not be anxious, saying, 'What shall we eat?' or 'What shall we drink?' or 'What shall we wear?' 32 For the Gentiles seek all these things; and your heavenly Father knows that you need them all. 33 But seek first his kingdom and his righteousness, and all these things shall be yours as well.

34 "Therefore do not be anxious about tomorrow, for tomorrow will be anxious for itself. Let the day's own trouble be sufficient for the day.

4.
=====

In Matthew 17, we learn about "Jesus and the Temple Tax."

24 When they came to Caper'na-um, the collectors of the half-shekel tax went up to Peter and said, "Does not your teacher pay the tax?" 25 He said, "Yes." And when he came home, Jesus spoke to him first, saying, "What do you think, Simon? From whom do kings of the earth take toll or tribute? From their sons or from others?" 26 And when he said, "From others," Jesus said to him, "Then the sons are free. 27 However, not to give offense to them, go to the sea and cast a hook, and take the first fish that comes up, and when you open its mouth you will find a shekel; take that and give it to them for me and for yourself."

5.
=====

In Matthew 19 (Mark 10, Luke 18), Jesus talks with "The Rich Young Man."

16 And behold, one came up to him, saying, "Teacher, what good deed must I do, to have eternal life?" 17 And he said to him, "Why do you ask me about what is good? One there is who is good. If you would enter life, keep the commandments." 18 He said to him, "Which?" And Jesus said, "You shall not kill, You shall not commit adultery, You shall not steal, You shall not bear false witness, 19 Honor your

father and mother, and, You shall love your neighbor as yourself." 20 The young man said to him, "All these I have observed; what do I still lack?" 21 Jesus said to him, "If you would be perfect, go, sell what you possess and give to the poor, and you will have treasure in heaven; and come, follow me." 22 When the young man heard this he went away sorrowful; for he had great possessions.

23 And Jesus said to his disciples, "Truly, I say to you, it will be hard for a rich man to enter the kingdom of heaven. 24 Again I tell you, it is easier for a camel to go through the eye of a needle than for a rich man to enter the kingdom of God." 25 When the disciples heard this they were greatly astonished, saying, "Who then can be saved?" 26 But Jesus looked at them and said to them, "With men this is impossible, but with God all things are possible." 27 Then Peter said in reply, "Lo, we have left everything and followed you. What then shall we have?" 28 Jesus said to them, "Truly, I say to you, in the new world, when the Son of man shall sit on his glorious throne, you who have followed me will also sit on twelve thrones, judging the twelve tribes of Israel. 29 And every one who has left houses or brothers or sisters or father or mother or children or lands, for my name's sake, will receive a hundredfold,[c] and inherit eternal life. 30 But many that are first will be last, and the last first.

6.
=====

In Matthew 22 (Mark 12, Luke 20), Jesus answers "The Question about Paying Taxes."

15 Then the Pharisees went and took counsel how to entangle him in his talk. 16 And they sent their disciples to him, along with the Hero'di-ans, saying, "Teacher, we know that you are true, and teach the way of God truthfully, and care for no man; for you do not regard the position of men. 17 Tell us, then, what you think. Is it lawful to pay taxes to Caesar, or not?" 18 But Jesus, aware of their malice, said, "Why put me to the test, you hypocrites? 19 Show me the money for the tax." And they brought him a coin.[a] 20 And Jesus said to them, "Whose likeness and inscription is this?" 21 They said, "Caesar's." Then he said to them, "Render therefore to Caesar the things that are Caesar's, and to God the things that are God's." 22 When they heard it, they marveled; and they left him and went away.

7.
=====

In Mark 12 (Luke 21), Jesus teaches about "The Widow's Offering."

41 And he sat down opposite the treasury, and watched the multitude putting money into the

treasury. Many rich people put in large sums. 42 And a poor widow came, and put in two copper coins, which make a penny. 43 And he called his disciples to him, and said to them, "Truly, I say to you, this poor widow has put in more than all those who are contributing to the treasury. 44 For they all contributed out of their abundance; but she out of her poverty has put in everything she had, her whole living."

8.
=====

In Luke 6 (Matthew 5), Jesus teaches about "Blessings and Woes."

20 And he lifted up his eyes on his disciples, and said: "Blessed are you poor, for yours is the kingdom of God.
21 "Blessed are you that hunger now, for you shall be satisfied.
"Blessed are you that weep now, for you shall laugh.
22 "Blessed are you when men hate you, and when they exclude you and revile you, and cast out your name as evil, on account of the Son of man! 23 Rejoice in that day, and leap for joy, for behold, your reward is great in heaven; for so their fathers did to the prophets.
24 "But woe to you that are rich, for you have received your consolation.

25 "Woe to you that are full now, for you shall hunger.

"Woe to you that laugh now, for you shall mourn and weep.

26 "Woe to you, when all men speak well of you, for so their fathers did to the false prophets.

9.
=====

In Luke 12, Jesus teaches "The Parable of the Rich Fool."

13 One of the multitude said to him, "Teacher, bid my brother divide the inheritance with me." 14 But he said to him, "Man, who made me a judge or divider over you?" 15 And he said to them, "Take heed, and beware of all covetousness [greediness]; for a man's life does not consist in the abundance of his possessions." 16 And he told them a parable, saying, "The land of a rich man brought forth plentifully; 17 and he thought to himself, 'What shall I do, for I have nowhere to store my crops?' 18 And he said, 'I will do this: I will pull down my barns, and build larger ones; and there I will store all my grain and my goods. 19 And I will say to my soul, Soul, you have ample goods laid up for many years; take your ease, eat, drink, be merry.' 20 But God said to him, 'Fool! This night your soul is required of you; and the things you have prepared, whose will they be?' 21 So is he

who lays up treasure for himself, and is not rich toward God."

10.
=====

In Luke 16, Jesus teaches "The Parable of the Dishonest Manager."

NOTE: [Mammon is a Semitic word for money or riches]

16 He also said to the disciples, "There was a rich man who had a steward, and charges were brought to him that this man was wasting his goods. 2 And he called him and said to him, 'What is this that I hear about you? Turn in the account of your stewardship, for you can no longer be steward.' 3 And the steward said to himself, 'What shall I do, since my master is taking the stewardship away from me? I am not strong enough to dig, and I am ashamed to beg. 4 I have decided what to do, so that people may receive me into their houses when I am put out of the stewardship.' 5 So, summoning his master's debtors one by one, he said to the first, 'How much do you owe my master?' 6 He said, 'A hundred measures of oil.' And he said to him, 'Take your bill, and sit down quickly and write fifty.' 7 Then he said to another, 'And how much do you owe?' He said, 'A hundred measures of wheat.' He said to him, 'Take your bill,

and write eighty.' 8 The master commended the dishonest steward for his shrewdness; for the sons of this world[a] are more shrewd in dealing with their own generation than the sons of light. 9 And I tell you, make friends for yourselves by means of unrighteous mammon,[b] so that when it fails they may receive you into the eternal habitations.
10 "He who is faithful in a very little is faithful also in much; and he who is dishonest in a very little is dishonest also in much. 11 If then you have not been faithful in the unrighteous mammon,[c] who will entrust to you the true riches? 12 And if you have not been faithful in that which is another's, who will give you that which is your own? 13 No servant can serve two masters; for either he will hate the one and love the other, or he will be devoted to the one and despise the other. You cannot serve God and mammon."[d]

11.
=====

In Luke 16, Jesus teaches about "The Law and the Kingdom of God."

14 The Pharisees, who were lovers of money, heard all this, and they scoffed at him. 15 But he said to them, "You are those who justify yourselves before men, but God knows your hearts; for what is exalted among men is an abomination in the sight of God.

16 "The law and the prophets were until John; since then the good news of the kingdom of God is preached, and every one enters it violently. 17 But it is easier for heaven and earth to pass away, than for one dot of the law to become void.

12.
=====

In Luke 16, Jesus teaches about "The Rich Man and Lazarus."

19 "There was a rich man, who was clothed in purple and fine linen and who feasted sumptuously every day. 20 And at his gate lay a poor man named Laz′arus, full of sores, 21 who desired to be fed with what fell from the rich man's table; moreover the dogs came and licked his sores. 22 The poor man died and was carried by the angels to Abraham's bosom. The rich man also died and was buried; 23 and in Hades, being in torment, he lifted up his eyes, and saw Abraham far off and Laz′arus in his bosom. 24 And he called out, 'Father Abraham, have mercy upon me, and send Laz′arus to dip the end of his finger in water and cool my tongue; for I am in anguish in this flame.' 25 But Abraham said, 'Son, remember that you in your lifetime received your good things, and Laz′arus in like manner evil things; but now he is comforted here, and you are in anguish. 26 And besides all this, between us and you a great

chasm has been fixed, in order that those who would pass from here to you may not be able, and none may cross from there to us.' 27 And he said, 'Then I beg you, father, to send him to my father's house, 28 for I have five brothers, so that he may warn them, lest they also come into this place of torment.' 29 But Abraham said, 'They have Moses and the prophets; let them hear them.' 30 And he said, 'No, father Abraham; but if some one goes to them from the dead, they will repent.' 31 He said to him, 'If they do not hear Moses and the prophets, neither will they be convinced if some one should rise from the dead.'"

(ii) Supporting Lessons on Money: 12 Passages

1.
=====

In Matthew 4 (Mark 1, Luke 4), we learn about "The Temptation of Jesus."

4 Then Jesus was led up by the Spirit into the wilderness to be tempted by the devil. 2 And he fasted forty days and forty nights, and afterward he was hungry. 3 And the tempter came and said to him, "If you are the Son of God, command these stones to

become loaves of bread." 4 But he answered, "It is written,
'Man shall not live by bread alone,
but by every word that proceeds from the mouth of God.'"
5 Then the devil took him to the holy city, and set him on the pinnacle of the temple, 6 and said to him, "If you are the Son of God, throw yourself down; for it is written,
'He will give his angels charge of you,'
and
'On their hands they will bear you up,
lest you strike your foot against a stone.'"
7 Jesus said to him, "Again it is written, 'You shall not tempt the Lord your God.'" 8 Again, the devil took him to a very high mountain, and showed him all the kingdoms of the world and the glory of them; 9 and he said to him, "All these I will give you, if you will fall down and worship me." 10 Then Jesus said to him, "Begone, Satan! for it is written,
'You shall worship the Lord your God
and him only shall you serve.'"
11 Then the devil left him, and behold, angels came and ministered to him.

2.
=====

In Matthew 10 (Mark 6, Luke 9), Jesus assigns "The Mission of the Twelve."

5 These twelve Jesus sent out, charging them, "Go nowhere among the Gentiles, and enter no town of the Samaritans, 6 but go rather to the lost sheep of the house of Israel. 7 And preach as you go, saying, 'The kingdom of heaven is at hand.' 8 Heal the sick, raise the dead, cleanse lepers, cast out demons. You received without paying, give without pay. 9 Take no gold, nor silver, nor copper in your belts, 10 no bag for your journey, nor two tunics, nor sandals, nor a staff; for the laborer deserves his food. 11 And whatever town or village you enter, find out who is worthy in it, and stay with him until you depart. 12 As you enter the house, salute it. 13 And if the house is worthy, let your peace come upon it; but if it is not worthy, let your peace return to you. 14 And if any one will not receive you or listen to your words, shake off the dust from your feet as you leave that house or town. 15 Truly, I say to you, it shall be more tolerable on the day of judgment for the land of Sodom and Gomor'rah than for that town.

3.
=====

In Matthew 21 (Mark 12, Luke 20), Jesus teaches "The Parable of the Wicked Tenants."

33 "Hear another parable. There was a householder who planted a vineyard, and set a hedge around it,

and dug a wine press in it, and built a tower, and let it out to tenants, and went into another country. 34 When the season of fruit drew near, he sent his servants to the tenants, to get his fruit; 35 and the tenants took his servants and beat one, killed another, and stoned another. 36 Again he sent other servants, more than the first; and they did the same to them. 37 Afterward he sent his son to them, saying, 'They will respect my son.' 38 But when the tenants saw the son, they said to themselves, 'This is the heir; come, let us kill him and have his inheritance.' 39 And they took him and cast him out of the vineyard, and killed him. 40 When therefore the owner of the vineyard comes, what will he do to those tenants?" 41 They said to him, "He will put those wretches to a miserable death, and let out the vineyard to other tenants who will give him the fruits in their seasons."

42 Jesus said to them, "Have you never read in the scriptures:

'The very stone which the builders rejected
has become the head of the corner;
this was the Lord's doing,
and it is marvelous in our eyes'?

43 Therefore I tell you, the kingdom of God will be taken away from you and given to a nation producing the fruits of it."[b]

45 When the chief priests and the Pharisees heard his parables, they perceived that he was speaking about them. 46 But when they tried to arrest him, they

feared the multitudes, because they held him to be a prophet.

4.
=====

In Matthew 25 (Luke 19), Jesus teaches "The Parable of the Talents."

14 "For it will be as when a man going on a journey called his servants and entrusted to them his property; 15 to one he gave five talents,[b] to another two, to another one, to each according to his ability. Then he went away. 16 He who had received the five talents went at once and traded with them; and he made five talents more. 17 So also, he who had the two talents made two talents more. 18 But he who had received the one talent went and dug in the ground and hid his master's money. 19 Now after a long time the master of those servants came and settled accounts with them. 20 And he who had received the five talents came forward, bringing five talents more, saying, 'Master, you delivered to me five talents; here I have made five talents more.' 21 His master said to him, 'Well done, good and faithful servant; you have been faithful over a little, I will set you over much; enter into the joy of your master.' 22 And he also who had the two talents came forward, saying, 'Master, you delivered to me two talents; here I have made two talents more.' 23 His master said to him, 'Well done,

good and faithful servant; you have been faithful over a little, I will set you over much; enter into the joy of your master.' 24 He also who had received the one talent came forward, saying, 'Master, I knew you to be a hard man, reaping where you did not sow, and gathering where you did not winnow; 25 so I was afraid, and I went and hid your talent in the ground. Here you have what is yours.' 26 But his master answered him, 'You wicked and slothful servant! You knew that I reap where I have not sowed, and gather where I have not winnowed? 27 Then you ought to have invested my money with the bankers, and at my coming I should have received what was my own with interest. 28 So take the talent from him, and give it to him who has the ten talents. 29 For to every one who has will more be given, and he will have abundance; but from him who has not, even what he has will be taken away. 30 And cast the worthless servant into the outer darkness; there men will weep and gnash their teeth.'

5.
=====

In Mathew 26 (Mark 14, Luke 22), we learn "Judas Agrees to Betray Jesus."

14 Then one of the twelve, who was called Judas Iscariot, went to the chief priests 15 and said, "What will you give me if I deliver him to you?" And they

paid him thirty pieces of silver. 16 And from that moment he sought an opportunity to betray him.

6.
=====

In Matthew 27, we learn about "The Suicide of Judas."

3 When Judas, his betrayer, saw that he was condemned, he repented and brought back the thirty pieces of silver to the chief priests and the elders, 4 saying, "I have sinned in betraying innocent blood." They said, "What is that to us? See to it yourself." 5 And throwing down the pieces of silver in the temple, he departed; and he went and hanged himself. 6 But the chief priests, taking the pieces of silver, said, "It is not lawful to put them into the treasury, since they are blood money." 7 So they took counsel, and bought with them the potter's field, to bury strangers in. 8 Therefore that field has been called the Field of Blood to this day. 9 Then was fulfilled what had been spoken by the prophet Jeremiah, saying, "And they took the thirty pieces of silver, the price of him on whom a price had been set by some of the sons of Israel, 10 and they gave them for the potter's field, as the Lord directed me."

7.

=====

In Luke 2, we learn about humble means through "The Birth of Jesus."

2 In those days a decree went out from Caesar Augustus that all the world should be enrolled. 2 This was the first enrollment, when Quirin′i-us was governor of Syria. 3 And all went to be enrolled, each to his own city. 4 And Joseph also went up from Galilee, from the city of Nazareth, to Judea, to the city of David, which is called Bethlehem, because he was of the house and lineage of David, 5 to be enrolled with Mary, his betrothed, who was with child. 6 And while they were there, the time came for her to be delivered. 7 And she gave birth to her first-born son and wrapped him in swaddling cloths, and laid him in a manger, because there was no place for them in the inn.

8.

=====

In Luke 2, we learn about the humble means of Jesus' birth with "The Shepherds and the Angels."

8 And in that region there were shepherds out in the field, keeping watch over their flock by night. 9 And an angel of the Lord appeared to them, and the glory of the Lord shone around them, and they were filled with fear. 10 And the angel said to them, "Be not

afraid; for behold, I bring you good news of a great joy which will come to all the people; 11 for to you is born this day in the city of David a Savior, who is Christ the Lord. 12 And this will be a sign for you: you will find a babe wrapped in swaddling cloths and lying in a manger." 13 And suddenly there was with the angel a multitude of the heavenly host praising God and saying,

14 "Glory to God in the highest,
and on earth peace among men with whom he is pleased!"[a]

15 When the angels went away from them into heaven, the shepherds said to one another, "Let us go over to Bethlehem and see this thing that has happened, which the Lord has made known to us." 16 And they went with haste, and found Mary and Joseph, and the babe lying in a manger. 17 And when they saw it they made known the saying which had been told them concerning this child; 18 and all who heard it wondered at what the shepherds told them. 19 But Mary kept all these things, pondering them in her heart. 20 And the shepherds returned, glorifying and praising God for all they had heard and seen, as it had been told them.

9.

=====

In Luke 9 (Mathew 8), Jesus teaches "Would-Be Followers of Jesus."

57 As they were going along the road, a man said to him, "I will follow you wherever you go." 58 And Jesus said to him, "Foxes have holes, and birds of the air have nests; but the Son of man has nowhere to lay his head." 59 To another he said, "Follow me." But he said, "Lord, let me first go and bury my father." 60 But he said to him, "Leave the dead to bury their own dead; but as for you, go and proclaim the kingdom of God." 61 Another said, "I will follow you, Lord; but let me first say farewell to those at my home." 62 Jesus said to him, "No one who puts his hand to the plow and looks back is fit for the kingdom of God."

10.
=====

In Luke 10, Jesus teaches about "The Mission of the Seventy."

10 After this the Lord appointed seventy[a] others, and sent them on ahead of him, two by two, into every town and place where he himself was about to come. 2 And he said to them, "The harvest is plentiful, but the laborers are few; pray therefore the Lord of the harvest to send out laborers into his harvest. 3 Go your way; behold, I send you out as lambs in the midst of wolves. 4 Carry no purse, no bag, no sandals; and salute no one on the road. 5 Whatever house you enter, first say, 'Peace be to this

house!' 6 And if a son of peace is there, your peace shall rest upon him; but if not, it shall return to you. 7 And remain in the same house, eating and drinking what they provide, for the laborer deserves his wages; do not go from house to house. 8 Whenever you enter a town and they receive you, eat what is set before you; 9 heal the sick in it and say to them, 'The kingdom of God has come near to you.' 10 But whenever you enter a town and they do not receive you, go into its streets and say, 11 'Even the dust of your town that clings to our feet, we wipe off against you; nevertheless know this, that the kingdom of God has come near.' 12 I tell you, it shall be more tolerable on that day for Sodom than for that town.

11.
=====

In Luke 14, Jesus teaches about "The Cost of Discipleship."

25 Now great multitudes accompanied him; and he turned and said to them, 26 "If any one comes to me and does not hate his own father and mother and wife and children and brothers and sisters, yes, and even his own life, he cannot be my disciple. 27 Whoever does not bear his own cross and come after me, cannot be my disciple. 28 For which of you, desiring to build a tower, does not first sit down and count the cost, whether he has enough to complete it? 29

Otherwise, when he has laid a foundation, and is not able to finish, all who see it begin to mock him, 30 saying, 'This man began to build, and was not able to finish.' 31 Or what king, going to encounter another king in war, will not sit down first and take counsel whether he is able with ten thousand to meet him who comes against him with twenty thousand? 32 And if not, while the other is yet a great way off, he sends an embassy and asks terms of peace. 33 So therefore, whoever of you does not renounce all that he has cannot be my disciple.

12.
=====

In Luke 22, Jesus teaches about "Purse, Bag, and Sword."

35 And he said to them, "When I sent you out with no purse or bag or sandals, did you lack anything?" They said, "Nothing." 36 He said to them, "But now, let him who has a purse take it, and likewise a bag. And let him who has no sword sell his mantle and buy one. 37 For I tell you that this scripture must be fulfilled in me, 'And he was reckoned with transgressors'; for what is written about me has its fulfilment." 38 And they said, "Look, Lord, here are two swords." And he said to them, "It is enough."

- Later on is "The Betrayal and Arrest of Jesus." Matthew 26 (Mark 14, Luke 22, John

18) reports: 47 While he was still speaking, Judas came, one of the twelve, and with him a great crowd with swords and clubs, from the chief priests and the elders of the people. 48 Now the betrayer had given them a sign, saying, "The one I shall kiss is the man; seize him." 49 And he came up to Jesus at once and said, "Hail, Master!"[g] And he kissed him. 50 Jesus said to him, "Friend, why are you here?"[h] Then they came up and laid hands on Jesus and seized him. *51 And behold, one of those who were with Jesus stretched out his hand and drew his sword, and struck the slave of the high priest, and cut off his ear. 52 Then Jesus said to him, "Put your sword back into its place; for all who take the sword will perish by the sword. 53 Do you think that I cannot appeal to my Father, and he will at once send me more than twelve legions of angels? 54 But how then should the scriptures be fulfilled, that it must be so?"* 55 At that hour Jesus said to the crowds, "Have you come out as against a robber, with swords and clubs to capture me? Day after day I sat in the temple teaching, and you did not seize me. 56 But all this has taken place, that the scriptures of the prophets might be fulfilled." Then all the disciples forsook him and fled.

(b) Lessons on Money from the Acts of the Apostles: 2 Passages

1.
=====

In Acts 2, we learn about "Life among the Believers."

43 And fear came upon every soul; and many wonders and signs were done through the apostles. 44 And all who believed were together and had all things in common; 45 and they sold their possessions and goods and distributed them to all, as any had need. 46 And day by day, attending the temple together and breaking bread in their homes, they partook of food with glad and generous hearts, 47 praising God and having favor with all the people. And the Lord added to their number day by day those who were being saved.

2.
=====

In Acts 4, we learn about how "The Believers Share Their Possessions."

32 Now the company of those who believed were of one heart and soul, and no one said that any of the things which he possessed was his own, but they had everything in common. 33 And with great power the apostles gave their testimony to the resurrection of the Lord Jesus, and great grace was upon them all. 34 There was not a needy person among them, for as many as were possessors of lands or houses sold them, and brought the proceeds of what was sold 35 and laid it at the apostles' feet; and distribution was made to each as any had need. 36 Thus Joseph who was surnamed by the apostles Barnabas (which means, Son of encouragement), a Levite, a native of Cyprus, 37 sold a field which belonged to him, and brought the money and laid it at the apostles' feet.

(c) **Lessons on Money from the Letters: 5 Passages**

These letters are mostly by Saint Paul, who is known as the Apostle to the Gentiles.

1.
=====

In 2 Corinthians 8, Paul teaches "Encouragement to Be Generous."

8 We want you to know, brethren, about the grace of God which has been shown in the churches of Macedo'nia, 2 for in a severe test of affliction, their abundance of joy and their extreme poverty have overflowed in a wealth of liberality on their part. 3 For they gave according to their means, as I can testify, and beyond their means, of their own free will, 4 begging us earnestly for the favor of taking part in the relief of the saints— 5 and this, not as we expected, but first they gave themselves to the Lord and to us by the will of God. 6 Accordingly we have urged Titus that as he had already made a beginning, he should also complete among you this gracious work. 7 Now as you excel in everything—in faith, in utterance, in knowledge, in all earnestness, and in your love for us—see that you excel in this gracious work also.

8 I say this not as a command, but to prove by the earnestness of others that your love also is genuine. 9 For you know the grace of our Lord Jesus Christ, that though he was rich, yet for your sake he became poor, so that by his poverty you might become rich. 10 And in this matter I give my advice: it is best for you now to complete what a year ago you began not only to do but to desire, 11 so that your readiness in desiring it may be matched by your completing it out of what you have. 12 For if the readiness is there, it is

acceptable according to what a man has, not according to what he has not. 13 I do not mean that others should be eased and you burdened, 14 but that as a matter of equality your abundance at the present time should supply their want, so that their abundance may supply your want, that there may be equality. 15 As it is written, "He who gathered much had nothing over, and he who gathered little had no lack."

2.
=====

In 1 Timothy 6, we are taught about "False Teaching and True Riches."

Teach and urge these duties. 3 If any one teaches otherwise and does not agree with the sound words of our Lord Jesus Christ and the teaching which accords with godliness, 4 he is puffed up with conceit, he knows nothing; he has a morbid craving for controversy and for disputes about words, which produce envy, dissension, slander, base suspicions, 5 and wrangling among men who are depraved in mind and bereft of the truth, imagining that godliness is a means of gain. 6 There is great gain in godliness with contentment; 7 for we brought nothing into the world, and[a] we cannot take anything out of the world; 8 but if we have food and clothing, with these we shall be content. 9 But those who desire to be rich fall into temptation, into a snare, into many senseless and hurtful desires that plunge men into ruin and destruction. 10 For the love of money is the root of all evils; it is through this craving that some have wandered away from the faith and pierced their hearts with many pangs.

3.
=====

In Hebrews 13, we are taught about "Service Well-Pleasing to God."

13 Let brotherly love continue. 2 Do not neglect to show hospitality to strangers, for thereby some have entertained angels unawares. 3 Remember those who are in prison, as though in prison with them; and those who are ill-treated, since you also are in the body. 4 Let marriage be held in honor among all, and let the marriage bed be undefiled; for God will judge the immoral and adulterous. 5 Keep your life free from love of money, and be content with what you have; for he has said, "I will never fail you nor forsake you." 6 Hence we can confidently say,
"The Lord is my helper,
I will not be afraid;
what can man do to me?"
7 Remember your leaders, those who spoke to you the word of God; consider the outcome of their life, and imitate their faith. 8 Jesus Christ is the same yesterday and today and for ever. 9 Do not be led

away by diverse and strange teachings; for it is well that the heart be strengthened by grace, not by foods, which have not benefited their adherents. 10 We have an altar from which those who serve the tent[a] have no right to eat. 11 For the bodies of those animals whose blood is brought into the sanctuary by the high priest as a sacrifice for sin are burned outside the camp. 12 So Jesus also suffered outside the gate in order to sanctify the people through his own blood. 13 Therefore let us go forth to him outside the camp, and bear the abuse he endured. 14 For here we have no lasting city, but we seek the city which is to come. 15 Through him then let us continually offer up a sacrifice of praise to God, that is, the fruit of lips that acknowledge his name. 16 Do not neglect to do good and to share what you have, for such sacrifices are pleasing to God.

17 Obey your leaders and submit to them; for they are keeping watch over your souls, as men who will have to give account. Let them do this joyfully, and not sadly, for that would be of no advantage to you.

18 Pray for us, for we are sure that we have a clear conscience, desiring to act honorably in all things. 19 I urge you the more earnestly to do this in order that I may be restored to you the sooner.

4.
=====

In James 1, we are taught about "Poverty and Riches."

9 Let the lowly brother boast in his exaltation, 10 and the rich in his humiliation, because like the flower of the grass he will pass away. 11 For the sun rises with its scorching heat and withers the grass; its flower falls, and its beauty perishes. So will the rich man fade away in the midst of his pursuits.

5.
=====

In James 5, we are taught about the "Warning to Rich Oppressors."

5 Come now, you rich, weep and howl for the miseries that are coming upon you. 2 Your riches have rotted and your garments are moth-eaten. 3 Your gold and silver have rusted, and their rust will be evidence against you and will eat your flesh like fire. You have laid up treasure[a] for the last days. 4 Behold, the wages of the laborers who mowed your fields, which you kept back by fraud, cry out; and the cries of the harvesters have reached the ears of the Lord of hosts. 5 You have lived on the earth in luxury and in pleasure; you have fattened your hearts in a day of slaughter. 6 You have condemned, you have killed the righteous man; he does not resist you.

(d) Lessons on Money from the Revelation to John: Notes

No passages.

(3)

SEX

This chapter contains a comprehensive collection of lessons on sex from Jesus and the New Testament.

It is important to recognize the various words in the New Testament that are associated with sex. These keywords include: pleasure, temptation, desire, lust, concupiscence, passion, flesh, fornication, impurity, defilement, immorality, chastity, abstinence, eunuch, virgin, marriage, adultery, divorce.

(a) **Lessons on Sex from Jesus in the Gospels: 13 Passages**

(i) Primary Lessons on Sex: 8 Passages

1-A.
=====

In Matthew 5 (Matthew 18, Mark 9), Jesus teaches "Concerning Adultery."

27 "You have heard that it was said, 'You shall not commit adultery.' 28 But I say to you that every one who looks at a woman lustfully has already committed adultery with her in his heart. 29 If your right eye causes you to sin, pluck it out and throw it away; it is better that you lose one of your members than that your whole body be thrown into hell.[d] 30 And if your right hand causes you to sin, cut it off and throw it away; it is better that you lose one of your members than that your whole body go into hell.[e]

1-B.
=====

In Matthew 18 (Matthew 5, Mark 9), Jesus teaches about "Temptations to Sin."

5 "Whoever receives one such child in my name receives me; 6 but whoever causes one of these little ones who believe in me to sin,[a] it would be better for him to have a great millstone fastened round his neck and to be drowned in the depth of the sea.

7 "Woe to the world for temptations to sin![b] For it is necessary that temptations come, but woe to the man by whom the temptation comes! 8 And if your hand or your foot causes you to sin,[c] cut it off and throw it away; it is better for you to enter life maimed or lame than with two hands or two feet to be thrown into the eternal fire.

[Passage ends with "your eye" Matthew 18:9; similar to Matthew 5:29 and Mark 9:47.]

1-C.
======

In Mark 9 (Matthew 5, Matthew 18), Jesus teaches about "Temptations to Sin."

[Passage begins with "these little ones" Mark 9:42; "your hand" Mark 9:43; "your foot" Mark 9:45; similar to Matthew 18:5-8.]

47 And if your eye causes you to sin,[n] pluck it out; it is better for you to enter the kingdom of God with one eye than with two eyes to be thrown into hell,[o] 48 where their worm does not die, and the fire is not quenched. 49 For every one will be salted with fire.[p] 50 Salt is good; but if the salt has lost its saltness, how will you season it? Have salt in yourselves, and be at peace with one another."

2.
=====

In Matthew 15 (Mark 7), Jesus teaches about "Things That Defile."

10 And he called the people to him and said to them, "Hear and understand: 11 not what goes into the mouth defiles a man, but what comes out of the mouth, this defiles a man." 12 Then the disciples came and said to him, "Do you know that the Pharisees were offended when they heard this saying?" 13 He answered, "Every plant which my heavenly Father has not planted will be rooted up. 14 Let them alone; they are blind guides. And if a blind man leads a blind man, both will fall into a pit." 15 But Peter said to him, "Explain the parable to us." 16 And he said, "Are you also still without understanding? 17 Do you not see that whatever goes into the mouth passes into the stomach, and so passes on?[c] 18 But what comes out of the mouth proceeds from the heart, and this defiles a man. 19 For out of the heart come evil thoughts, murder, adultery, fornication, theft, false witness, slander. 20 These are what defile a man; but to eat with unwashed hands does not defile a man."

3.
=====

In Matthew 19 (Matthew 5, Mark 10, Luke 16), Jesus gives a "Teaching about Divorce."

3 And Pharisees came up to him and tested him by asking, "Is it lawful to divorce one's wife for any cause?" 4 He answered, "Have you not read that he who made them from the beginning made them male and female, 5 and said, 'For this reason a man shall leave his father and mother and be joined to his wife, and the two shall become one flesh'? 6 So they are no longer two but one flesh. What therefore God has joined together, let not man put asunder." 7 They said to him, "Why then did Moses command one to give a certificate of divorce, and to put her away?" 8 He said to them, "For your hardness of heart Moses allowed you to divorce your wives, but from the beginning it was not so. 9 And I say to you: whoever divorces his wife, except for unchastity,[a] and marries another, commits adultery."[b]
10 The disciples said to him, "If such is the case of a man with his wife, it is not expedient to marry." 11 But he said to them, "Not all men can receive this saying, but only those to whom it is given. 12 For there are eunuchs who have been so from birth, and there are eunuchs who have been made eunuchs by men, and there are eunuchs who have made themselves eunuchs for the sake of the kingdom of heaven. He who is able to receive this, let him receive it."

4.

=====

In Matthew 25, Jesus teaches "The Parable of the Ten Bridesmaids."

25 "Then the kingdom of heaven shall be compared to ten maidens who took their lamps and went to meet the bridegroom.[a] 2 Five of them were foolish, and five were wise. 3 For when the foolish took their lamps, they took no oil with them; 4 but the wise took flasks of oil with their lamps. 5 As the bridegroom was delayed, they all slumbered and slept. 6 But at midnight there was a cry, 'Behold, the bridegroom! Come out to meet him.' 7 Then all those maidens rose and trimmed their lamps. 8 And the foolish said to the wise, 'Give us some of your oil, for our lamps are going out.' 9 But the wise replied, 'Perhaps there will not be enough for us and for you; go rather to the dealers and buy for yourselves.' 10 And while they went to buy, the bridegroom came, and those who were ready went in with him to the marriage feast; and the door was shut. 11 Afterward the other maidens came also, saying, 'Lord, lord, open to us.' 12 But he replied, 'Truly, I say to you, I do not know you.' 13 Watch therefore, for you know neither the day nor the hour.

5.

=====

In Luke 11, Jesus teaches about "The Return of the Unclean Spirit."

24 "When the unclean spirit has gone out of a man, he passes through waterless places seeking rest; and finding none he says, 'I will return to my house from which I came.' 25 And when he comes he finds it swept and put in order. 26 Then he goes and brings seven other spirits more evil than himself, and they enter and dwell there; and the last state of that man becomes worse than the first."

6.

=====

In Luke 15, Jesus teaches "The Parable of the Prodigal and His Brother."

11 And he said, "There was a man who had two sons; 12 and the younger of them said to his father, 'Father, give me the share of property that falls to me.' And he divided his living between them. 13 Not many days later, the younger son gathered all he had and took his journey into a far country, and there he squandered his property in loose living. 14 And when he had spent everything, a great famine arose in that country, and he began to be in want. 15 So he went and joined himself to one of the citizens of that country, who sent him into his fields to feed swine. 16 And he

would gladly have fed on[b] the pods that the swine ate; and no one gave him anything. 17 But when he came to himself he said, 'How many of my father's hired servants have bread enough and to spare, but I perish here with hunger! 18 I will arise and go to my father, and I will say to him, "Father, I have sinned against heaven and before you; 19 I am no longer worthy to be called your son; treat me as one of your hired servants."' 20 And he arose and came to his father. But while he was yet at a distance, his father saw him and had compassion, and ran and embraced him and kissed him. 21 And the son said to him, 'Father, I have sinned against heaven and before you; I am no longer worthy to be called your son.'[c] 22 But the father said to his servants, 'Bring quickly the best robe, and put it on him; and put a ring on his hand, and shoes on his feet; 23 and bring the fatted calf and kill it, and let us eat and make merry; 24 for this my son was dead, and is alive again; he was lost, and is found.' And they began to make merry.

25 "Now his elder son was in the field; and as he came and drew near to the house, he heard music and dancing. 26 And he called one of the servants and asked what this meant. 27 And he said to him, 'Your brother has come, and your father has killed the fatted calf, because he has received him safe and sound.' 28 But he was angry and refused to go in. His father came out and entreated him, 29 but he answered his father, 'Lo, these many years I have served you, and I never disobeyed your command; yet you never gave

me a kid, that I might make merry with my friends. 30 But when this son of yours came, who has devoured your living with harlots, you killed for him the fatted calf!' 31 And he said to him, 'Son, you are always with me, and all that is mine is yours. 32 It was fitting to make merry and be glad, for this your brother was dead, and is alive; he was lost, and is found.'"

7.
=====

In John 7-8, Jesus talks with "The Woman Caught in Adultery."

53 They went each to his own house,
8 1 but Jesus went to the Mount of Olives. 2 Early in the morning he came again to the temple; all the people came to him, and he sat down and taught them. 3 The scribes and the Pharisees brought a woman who had been caught in adultery, and placing her in the midst 4 they said to him, "Teacher, this woman has been caught in the act of adultery. 5 Now in the law Moses commanded us to stone such. What do you say about her?" 6 This they said to test him, that they might have some charge to bring against him. Jesus bent down and wrote with his finger on the ground. 7 And as they continued to ask him, he stood up and said to them, "Let him who is without sin among you be the first to throw a stone at her." 8 And

once more he bent down and wrote with his finger on the ground. 9 But when they heard it, they went away, one by one, beginning with the eldest, and Jesus was left alone with the woman standing before him. 10 Jesus looked up and said to her, "Woman, where are they? Has no one condemned you?" 11 She said, "No one, Lord." And Jesus said, "Neither do I condemn you; go, and do not sin again."[a]

8.
=====

In John 8, Jesus teaches about "True Disciples."

31 Jesus then said to the Jews who had believed in him, "If you continue in my word, you are truly my disciples, 32 and you will know the truth, and the truth will make you free." 33 They answered him, "We are descendants of Abraham, and have never been in bondage to any one. How is it that you say, 'You will be made free'?"
34 Jesus answered them, "Truly, truly, I say to you, every one who commits sin is a slave to sin. 35 The slave does not continue in the house for ever; the son continues for ever. 36 So if the Son makes you free, you will be free indeed. 37 I know that you are descendants of Abraham; yet you seek to kill me, because my word finds no place in you. 38 I speak of what I have seen with my Father, and you do what you have heard from your father."

(ii) Supporting Lessons on Sex: 5 Passages

1.
=====

In Matthew 1, we learn about "The Birth of Jesus the Messiah."

18 Now the birth of Jesus Christ[i] took place in this way. When his mother Mary had been betrothed to Joseph, before they came together she was found to be with child of the Holy Spirit; 19 and her husband Joseph, being a just man and unwilling to put her to shame, resolved to divorce her quietly. 20 But as he considered this, behold, an angel of the Lord appeared to him in a dream, saying, "Joseph, son of David, do not fear to take Mary your wife, for that which is conceived in her is of the Holy Spirit; 21 she will bear a son, and you shall call his name Jesus, for he will save his people from their sins." 22 All this took place to fulfil what the Lord had spoken by the prophet:
23 "Behold, a virgin shall conceive and bear a son, and his name shall be called Emman'u-el"
(which means, God with us). 24 When Joseph woke from sleep, he did as the angel of the Lord

commanded him; he took his wife, 25 but knew her not until she had borne a son; and he called his name Jesus.

In Luke, the circumstances of Jesus' birth are described with additional detail:

+ Luke 1. The Birth of John the Baptist Foretold
+ Luke 1. The Birth of Jesus Foretold
+ Luke 1. Mary Visits Elizabeth
+ Luke 1. Mary's Song of Praise
+ Luke 1. The Birth of John the Baptist
+ Luke 1. Zechariah's Prophecy
+ Luke 2. The Birth of Jesus

2.
=====

In Matthew 22, Jesus teaches "The Parable of the Wedding Banquet."

22 And again Jesus spoke to them in parables, saying, 2 "The kingdom of heaven may be compared to a king who gave a marriage feast for his son, 3 and sent his servants to call those who were invited to the marriage feast; but they would not come. 4 Again he sent other servants, saying, 'Tell those who are invited, Behold, I have made ready my dinner, my oxen and my fat calves are killed, and everything is

ready; come to the marriage feast.' 5 But they made light of it and went off, one to his farm, another to his business, 6 while the rest seized his servants, treated them shamefully, and killed them. 7 The king was angry, and he sent his troops and destroyed those murderers and burned their city. 8 Then he said to his servants, 'The wedding is ready, but those invited were not worthy. 9 Go therefore to the thoroughfares, and invite to the marriage feast as many as you find.' 10 And those servants went out into the streets and gathered all whom they found, both bad and good; so the wedding hall was filled with guests.

11 "But when the king came in to look at the guests, he saw there a man who had no wedding garment; 12 and he said to him, 'Friend, how did you get in here without a wedding garment?' And he was speechless. 13 Then the king said to the attendants, 'Bind him hand and foot, and cast him into the outer darkness; there men will weep and gnash their teeth.' 14 For many are called, but few are chosen."

3.
=====

In Matthew 24 (Mark 13, Luke 21), Jesus teaches about "The Desolating Sacrilege."

15 "So when you see the desolating sacrilege spoken of by the prophet Daniel, standing in the holy place (let the reader understand), 16 then let those who are

in Judea flee to the mountains; 17 let him who is on the housetop not go down to take what is in his house; 18 and let him who is in the field not turn back to take his mantle. 19 And alas for those who are with child and for those who give suck in those days! 20 Pray that your flight may not be in winter or on a sabbath. 21 For then there will be great tribulation, such as has not been from the beginning of the world until now, no, and never will be. 22 And if those days had not been shortened, no human being would be saved; but for the sake of the elect those days will be shortened. 23 Then if any one says to you, 'Lo, here is the Christ!' or 'There he is!' do not believe it. 24 For false Christs and false prophets will arise and show great signs and wonders, so as to lead astray, if possible, even the elect. 25 Lo, I have told you beforehand. 26 So, if they say to you, 'Lo, he is in the wilderness,' do not go out; if they say, 'Lo, he is in the inner rooms,' do not believe it. 27 For as the lightning comes from the east and shines as far as the west, so will be the coming of the Son of man. 28 Wherever the body is, there the eagles[b] will be gathered together.

4.
=====

In Matthew 24 (Mark 13, Luke 21), Jesus teaches about "The Necessity for Watchfulness."

36 "But of that day and hour no one knows, not even the angels of heaven, nor the Son,[c] but the Father only. 37 As were the days of Noah, so will be the coming of the Son of man. 38 For as in those days before the flood they were eating and drinking, marrying and giving in marriage, until the day when Noah entered the ark, 39 and they did not know until the flood came and swept them all away, so will be the coming of the Son of man. 40 Then two men will be in the field; one is taken and one is left. 41 Two women will be grinding at the mill; one is taken and one is left. 42 Watch therefore, for you do not know on what day your Lord is coming. 43 But know this, that if the householder had known in what part of the night the thief was coming, he would have watched and would not have let his house be broken into. 44 Therefore you also must be ready; for the Son of man is coming at an hour you do not expect.

5.
=====

In Luke 7, we learn about "A Sinful Woman Forgiven."

36 One of the Pharisees asked him to eat with him, and he went into the Pharisee's house, and took his place at table. 37 And behold, a woman of the city, who was a sinner, when she learned that he was at table in the Pharisee's house, brought an alabaster

flask of ointment, 38 and standing behind him at his feet, weeping, she began to wet his feet with her tears, and wiped them with the hair of her head, and kissed his feet, and anointed them with the ointment. 39 Now when the Pharisee who had invited him saw it, he said to himself, "If this man were a prophet, he would have known who and what sort of woman this is who is touching him, for she is a sinner." 40 And Jesus answering said to him, "Simon, I have something to say to you." And he answered, "What is it, Teacher?" 41 "A certain creditor had two debtors; one owed five hundred denarii, and the other fifty. 42 When they could not pay, he forgave them both. Now which of them will love him more?" 43 Simon answered, "The one, I suppose, to whom he forgave more." And he said to him, "You have judged rightly." 44 Then turning toward the woman he said to Simon, "Do you see this woman? I entered your house, you gave me no water for my feet, but she has wet my feet with her tears and wiped them with her hair. 45 You gave me no kiss, but from the time I came in she has not ceased to kiss my feet. 46 You did not anoint my head with oil, but she has anointed my feet with ointment. 47 Therefore I tell you, her sins, which are many, are forgiven, for she loved much; but he who is forgiven little, loves little." 48 And he said to her, "Your sins are forgiven." 49 Then those who were at table with him began to say among themselves, "Who is this, who even forgives sins?"

50 And he said to the woman, "Your faith has saved you; go in peace."

(b) <u>**Lessons on Sex from the Acts of the Apostles: Notes**</u>

No passages.

(c) <u>**Lessons on Sex from the Letters: 18 Passages**</u>

These letters are mostly by Saint Paul, who is known as the Apostle to the Gentiles.

1.
=====

In Romans 1, Paul teaches about "The Guilt of Mankind."

18 For the wrath of God is revealed from heaven against all ungodliness and wickedness of men who

by their wickedness suppress the truth. 19 For what can be known about God is plain to them, because God has shown it to them. 20 Ever since the creation of the world his invisible nature, namely, his eternal power and deity, has been clearly perceived in the things that have been made. So they are without excuse; 21 for although they knew God they did not honor him as God or give thanks to him, but they became futile in their thinking and their senseless minds were darkened. 22 Claiming to be wise, they became fools, 23 and exchanged the glory of the immortal God for images resembling mortal man or birds or animals or reptiles.

24 Therefore God gave them up in the lusts of their hearts to impurity, to the dishonoring of their bodies among themselves, 25 because they exchanged the truth about God for a lie and worshiped and served the creature rather than the Creator, who is blessed for ever! Amen.

26 For this reason God gave them up to dishonorable passions. Their women exchanged natural relations for unnatural, 27 and the men likewise gave up natural relations with women and were consumed with passion for one another, men committing shameless acts with men and receiving in their own persons the due penalty for their error.

28 And since they did not see fit to acknowledge God, God gave them up to a base mind and to improper conduct. 29 They were filled with all manner of wickedness, evil, covetousness, malice.

Full of envy, murder, strife, deceit, malignity, they are gossips, 30 slanderers, haters of God, insolent, haughty, boastful, inventors of evil, disobedient to parents, 31 foolish, faithless, heartless, ruthless. 32 Though they know God's decree that those who do such things deserve to die, they not only do them but approve those who practice them.

2.
=====

In Romans 7, Paul teaches "An Analogy from Marriage."

7 Do you not know, brethren—for I am speaking to those who know the law—that the law is binding on a person only during his life? 2 Thus a married woman is bound by law to her husband as long as he lives; but if her husband dies she is discharged from the law concerning the husband. 3 Accordingly, she will be called an adulteress if she lives with another man while her husband is alive. But if her husband dies she is free from that law, and if she marries another man she is not an adulteress.
4 Likewise, my brethren, you have died to the law through the body of Christ, so that you may belong to another, to him who has been raised from the dead in order that we may bear fruit for God. 5 While we were living in the flesh, our sinful passions, aroused by the law, were at work in our members to bear fruit

for death. 6 But now we are discharged from the law, dead to that which held us captive, so that we serve not under the old written code but in the new life of the Spirit.

3.
=====

In 1 Corinthians 5, Paul teaches that "Sexual Immorality Defiles the Church."

5 It is actually reported that there is immorality among you, and of a kind that is not found even among pagans; for a man is living with his father's wife. 2 And you are arrogant! Ought you not rather to mourn? Let him who has done this be removed from among you.
3 For though absent in body I am present in spirit, and as if present, I have already pronounced judgment 4 in the name of the Lord Jesus on the man who has done such a thing. When you are assembled, and my spirit is present, with the power of our Lord Jesus, 5 you are to deliver this man to Satan for the destruction of the flesh, that his spirit may be saved in the day of the Lord Jesus.[a]
6 Your boasting is not good. Do you not know that a little leaven leavens the whole lump? 7 Cleanse out the old leaven that you may be a new lump, as you really are unleavened. For Christ, our paschal lamb, has been sacrificed. 8 Let us, therefore, celebrate the

festival, not with the old leaven, the leaven of malice and evil, but with the unleavened bread of sincerity and truth.

4.
=====

In 1 Corinthians 5, Paul teaches that "Sexual Immorality Must Be Judged."

9 I wrote to you in my letter not to associate with immoral men; 10 not at all meaning the immoral of this world, or the greedy and robbers, or idolaters, since then you would need to go out of the world. 11 But rather I wrote[b] to you not to associate with any one who bears the name of brother if he is guilty of immorality or greed, or is an idolater, reviler, drunkard, or robber—not even to eat with such a one. 12 For what have I to do with judging outsiders? Is it not those inside the church whom you are to judge? 13 God judges those outside. "Drive out the wicked person from among you."

5.
=====

In 1 Corinthians 6, Paul teaches to "Glorify God in Body and Spirit."

12 "All things are lawful for me," but not all things are helpful. "All things are lawful for me," but I will not be enslaved by anything. 13 "Food is meant for the stomach and the stomach for food"—and God will destroy both one and the other. The body is not meant for immorality, but for the Lord, and the Lord for the body. 14 And God raised the Lord and will also raise us up by his power. 15 Do you not know that your bodies are members of Christ? Shall I therefore take the members of Christ and make them members of a prostitute? Never! 16 Do you not know that he who joins himself to a prostitute becomes one body with her? For, as it is written, "The two shall become one flesh." 17 But he who is united to the Lord becomes one spirit with him. 18 Shun immorality. Every other sin which a man commits is outside the body; but the immoral man sins against his own body. 19 Do you not know that your body is a temple of the Holy Spirit within you, which you have from God? You are not your own; 20 you were bought with a price. So glorify God in your body.

6.
=====

In 1 Corinthians 7, Paul teaches "Directions concerning Marriage."

7 Now concerning the matters about which you wrote. It is well for a man not to touch a woman. 2

But because of the temptation to immorality, each man should have his own wife and each woman her own husband. 3 The husband should give to his wife her conjugal rights, and likewise the wife to her husband. 4 For the wife does not rule over her own body, but the husband does; likewise the husband does not rule over his own body, but the wife does. 5 Do not refuse one another except perhaps by agreement for a season, that you may devote yourselves to prayer; but then come together again, lest Satan tempt you through lack of self-control. 6 I say this by way of concession, not of command. 7 I wish that all were as I myself am. But each has his own special gift from God, one of one kind and one of another.

8 To the unmarried and the widows I say that it is well for them to remain single as I do. 9 But if they cannot exercise self-control, they should marry. For it is better to marry than to be aflame with passion. 10 To the married I give charge, not I but the Lord, that the wife should not separate from her husband 11 (but if she does, let her remain single or else be reconciled to her husband)—and that the husband should not divorce his wife.

12 To the rest I say, not the Lord, that if any brother has a wife who is an unbeliever, and she consents to live with him, he should not divorce her. 13 If any woman has a husband who is an unbeliever, and he consents to live with her, she should not divorce him. 14 For the unbelieving husband is consecrated

through his wife, and the unbelieving wife is consecrated through her husband. Otherwise, your children would be unclean, but as it is they are holy. 15 But if the unbelieving partner desires to separate, let it be so; in such a case the brother or sister is not bound. For God has called us[a] to peace. 16 Wife, how do you know whether you will save your husband? Husband, how do you know whether you will save your wife?

7.
=====

1 Corinthians 7, Paul teaches about the "The Unmarried and the Widows."

25 Now concerning the unmarried,[c] I have no command of the Lord, but I give my opinion as one who by the Lord's mercy is trustworthy. 26 I think that in view of the present[d] distress it is well for a person to remain as he is. 27 Are you bound to a wife? Do not seek to be free. Are you free from a wife? Do not seek marriage. 28 But if you marry, you do not sin, and if a girl[e] marries she does not sin. Yet those who marry will have worldly troubles, and I would spare you that. 29 I mean, brethren, the appointed time has grown very short; from now on, let those who have wives live as though they had none, 30 and those who mourn as though they were not mourning, and those who rejoice as though they

were not rejoicing, and those who buy as though they had no goods, 31 and those who deal with the world as though they had no dealings with it. For the form of this world is passing away.

32 I want you to be free from anxieties. The unmarried man is anxious about the affairs of the Lord, how to please the Lord; 33 but the married man is anxious about worldly affairs, how to please his wife, 34 and his interests are divided. And the unmarried woman or girl[f] is anxious about the affairs of the Lord, how to be holy in body and spirit; but the married woman is anxious about worldly affairs, how to please her husband. 35 I say this for your own benefit, not to lay any restraint upon you, but to promote good order and to secure your undivided devotion to the Lord.

36 If any one thinks that he is not behaving properly toward his betrothed,[g] if his passions are strong, and it has to be, let him do as he wishes: let them marry—it is no sin. 37 But whoever is firmly established in his heart, being under no necessity but having his desire under control, and has determined this in his heart, to keep her as his betrothed,[h] he will do well. 38 So that he who marries his betrothed[i] does well; and he who refrains from marriage will do better.

39 A wife is bound to her husband as long as he lives. If the husband dies, she is free to be married to whom she wishes, only in the Lord. 40 But in my judgment she is happier if she remains as she is. And I think that I have the Spirit of God.

8.
=====

In 2 Corinthians 6-7, Paul teaches about the "The Temple of the Living God."

14 Do not be mismated with unbelievers. For what partnership have righteousness and iniquity? Or what fellowship has light with darkness? 15 What accord has Christ with Be'lial?[a] Or what has a believer in common with an unbeliever? 16 What agreement has the temple of God with idols? For we are the temple of the living God; as God said,
"I will live in them and move among them,
and I will be their God,
and they shall be my people.
17 Therefore come out from them,
and be separate from them, says the Lord,
and touch nothing unclean;
then I will welcome you,
18 and I will be a father to you,
and you shall be my sons and daughters,
says the Lord Almighty."
7 Since we have these promises, beloved, let us cleanse ourselves from every defilement of body and spirit, and make holiness perfect in the fear of God.

9.

=====

In Galatians 5, Paul teaches about "The Works of the Flesh and the Fruit of the Spirit."

16 But I say, walk by the Spirit, and do not gratify the desires of the flesh. 17 For the desires of the flesh are against the Spirit, and the desires of the Spirit are against the flesh; for these are opposed to each other, to prevent you from doing what you would. 18 But if you are led by the Spirit you are not under the law. 19 Now the works of the flesh are plain: fornication, impurity, licentiousness, 20 idolatry, sorcery, enmity, strife, jealousy, anger, selfishness, dissension, party spirit, 21 envy,[b] drunkenness, carousing, and the like. I warn you, as I warned you before, that those who do such things shall not inherit the kingdom of God. 22 But the fruit of the Spirit is love, joy, peace, patience, kindness, goodness, faithfulness, 23 gentleness, self-control; against such there is no law. 24 And those who belong to Christ Jesus have crucified the flesh with its passions and desires. 25 If we live by the Spirit, let us also walk by the Spirit. 26 Let us have no self-conceit, no provoking of one another, no envy of one another.

10.
=====

In Ephesians 5, Paul teaches to "Renounce Pagan Ways."

3 But fornication and all impurity or covetousness must not even be named among you, as is fitting among saints. 4 Let there be no filthiness, nor silly talk, nor levity, which are not fitting; but instead let there be thanksgiving. 5 Be sure of this, that no fornicator or impure man, or one who is covetous (that is, an idolater), has any inheritance in the kingdom of Christ and of God. 6 Let no one deceive you with empty words, for it is because of these things that the wrath of God comes upon the sons of disobedience. 7 Therefore do not associate with them, 8 for once you were darkness, but now you are light in the Lord; walk as children of light 9 (for the fruit of light is found in all that is good and right and true), 10 and try to learn what is pleasing to the Lord. 11 Take no part in the unfruitful works of darkness, but instead expose them. 12 For it is a shame even to speak of the things that they do in secret; 13 but when anything is exposed by the light it becomes visible, for anything that becomes visible is light. 14 Therefore it is said,

"Awake, O sleeper, and arise from the dead, and Christ shall give you light."

15 Look carefully then how you walk, not as unwise men but as wise, 16 making the most of the time, because the days are evil. 17 Therefore do not be foolish, but understand what the will of the Lord is. 18 And do not get drunk with wine, for that is debauchery; but be filled with the Spirit, 19

addressing one another in psalms and hymns and spiritual songs, singing and making melody to the Lord with all your heart, 20 always and for everything giving thanks in the name of our Lord Jesus Christ to God the Father.

11.
=====

In Ephesians 5, Paul teaches about "The Christian Household."

21 Be subject to one another out of reverence for Christ. 22 Wives, be subject to your husbands, as to the Lord. 23 For the husband is the head of the wife as Christ is the head of the church, his body, and is himself its Savior. 24 As the church is subject to Christ, so let wives also be subject in everything to their husbands. 25 Husbands, love your wives, as Christ loved the church and gave himself up for her, 26 that he might sanctify her, having cleansed her by the washing of water with the word, 27 that he might present the church to himself in splendor, without spot or wrinkle or any such thing, that she might be holy and without blemish. 28 Even so husbands should love their wives as their own bodies. He who loves his wife loves himself. 29 For no man ever hates his own flesh, but nourishes and cherishes it, as Christ does the church, 30 because we are members of his body. 31 "For this reason a man shall leave his

father and mother and be joined to his wife, and the two shall become one flesh." 32 This mystery is a profound one, and I am saying that it refers to Christ and the church; 33 however, let each one of you love his wife as himself, and let the wife see that she respects her husband.

12.
=====

In 1 Thessalonians 4, Paul teaches about "A Life Pleasing to God."

4 Finally, brethren, we beseech and exhort you in the Lord Jesus, that as you learned from us how you ought to live and to please God, just as you are doing, you do so more and more. 2 For you know what instructions we gave you through the Lord Jesus. 3 For this is the will of God, your sanctification: that you abstain from unchastity; 4 that each one of you know how to take a wife for himself[a] in holiness and honor, 5 not in the passion of lust like heathen who do not know God; 6 that no man transgress, and wrong his brother in this matter,[b] because the Lord is an avenger in all these things, as we solemnly forewarned you. 7 For God has not called us for uncleanness, but in holiness. 8 Therefore whoever disregards this, disregards not man but God, who gives his Holy Spirit to you.

9 But concerning love of the brethren you have no need to have any one write to you, for you yourselves have been taught by God to love one another; 10 and indeed you do love all the brethren throughout Macedo′nia. But we exhort you, brethren, to do so more and more, 11 to aspire to live quietly, to mind your own affairs, and to work with your hands, as we charged you; 12 so that you may command the respect of outsiders, and be dependent on nobody.

13.
=====

In 1 Timothy 2, we are taught "Instructions concerning Prayer."

2 First of all, then, I urge that supplications, prayers, intercessions, and thanksgivings be made for all men, 2 for kings and all who are in high positions, that we may lead a quiet and peaceable life, godly and respectful in every way. 3 This is good, and it is acceptable in the sight of God our Savior, 4 who desires all men to be saved and to come to the knowledge of the truth. 5 For there is one God, and there is one mediator between God and men, the man Christ Jesus, 6 who gave himself as a ransom for all, the testimony to which was borne at the proper time. 7 For this I was appointed a preacher and apostle (I am telling the truth, I am not lying), a teacher of the Gentiles in faith and truth.

8 I desire then that in every place the men should pray, lifting holy hands without anger or quarreling; 9 also that women should adorn themselves modestly and sensibly in seemly apparel, not with braided hair or gold or pearls or costly attire 10 but by good deeds, as befits women who profess religion. 11 Let a woman learn in silence with all submissiveness. 12 I permit no woman to teach or to have authority over men; she is to keep silent. 13 For Adam was formed first, then Eve; 14 and Adam was not deceived, but the woman was deceived and became a transgressor. 15 Yet woman will be saved through bearing children,[a] if she continues[b] in faith and love and holiness, with modesty.

14.
=====

In Hebrews 13, we are taught about "Service Well-Pleasing to God."

13 Let brotherly love continue. 2 Do not neglect to show hospitality to strangers, for thereby some have entertained angels unawares. 3 Remember those who are in prison, as though in prison with them; and those who are ill-treated, since you also are in the body. 4 Let marriage be held in honor among all, and let the marriage bed be undefiled; for God will judge the immoral and adulterous. 5 Keep your life free from love of money, and be content with what you

have; for he has said, "I will never fail you nor forsake you." 6 Hence we can confidently say,
"The Lord is my helper,
I will not be afraid;
what can man do to me?"
7 Remember your leaders, those who spoke to you the word of God; consider the outcome of their life, and imitate their faith. 8 Jesus Christ is the same yesterday and today and for ever. 9 Do not be led away by diverse and strange teachings; for it is well that the heart be strengthened by grace, not by foods, which have not benefited their adherents. 10 We have an altar from which those who serve the tent[a] have no right to eat. 11 For the bodies of those animals whose blood is brought into the sanctuary by the high priest as a sacrifice for sin are burned outside the camp. 12 So Jesus also suffered outside the gate in order to sanctify the people through his own blood. 13 Therefore let us go forth to him outside the camp, and bear the abuse he endured. 14 For here we have no lasting city, but we seek the city which is to come. 15 Through him then let us continually offer up a sacrifice of praise to God, that is, the fruit of lips that acknowledge his name. 16 Do not neglect to do good and to share what you have, for such sacrifices are pleasing to God.
17 Obey your leaders and submit to them; for they are keeping watch over your souls, as men who will have to give account. Let them do this joyfully, and not sadly, for that would be of no advantage to you.

18 Pray for us, for we are sure that we have a clear conscience, desiring to act honorably in all things. 19 I urge you the more earnestly to do this in order that I may be restored to you the sooner.

15.
=====

In James 1, we are taught about "Trial and Temptation."

12 Blessed is the man who endures trial, for when he has stood the test he will receive the crown of life which God has promised to those who love him. 13 Let no one say when he is tempted, "I am tempted by God"; for God cannot be tempted with evil and he himself tempts no one; 14 but each person is tempted when he is lured and enticed by his own desire. 15 Then desire when it has conceived gives birth to sin; and sin when it is full-grown brings forth death. 16 Do not be deceived, my beloved brethren. 17 Every good endowment and every perfect gift is from above, coming down from the Father of lights with whom there is no variation or shadow due to change.[a] 18 Of his own will he brought us forth by the word of truth that we should be a kind of first fruits of his creatures.

16.

Becoming God-like | JTA

=====

In 1 Peter 2, we are taught to "Live as Servants of God."

11 Beloved, I beseech you as aliens and exiles to abstain from the passions of the flesh that wage war against your soul. 12 Maintain good conduct among the Gentiles, so that in case they speak against you as wrongdoers, they may see your good deeds and glorify God on the day of visitation.
13 Be subject for the Lord's sake to every human institution,[b] whether it be to the emperor as supreme, 14 or to governors as sent by him to punish those who do wrong and to praise those who do right. 15 For it is God's will that by doing right you should put to silence the ignorance of foolish men. 16 Live as free men, yet without using your freedom as a pretext for evil; but live as servants of God. 17 Honor all men. Love the brotherhood. Fear God. Honor the emperor.

17.
=====

In 1 Peter 3, we are taught about "Wives and Husbands."

3 Likewise you wives, be submissive to your husbands, so that some, though they do not obey the word, may be won without a word by the behavior of

their wives, 2 when they see your reverent and chaste behavior. 3 Let not yours be the outward adorning with braiding of hair, decoration of gold, and wearing of fine clothing, 4 but let it be the hidden person of the heart with the imperishable jewel of a gentle and quiet spirit, which in God's sight is very precious. 5 So once the holy women who hoped in God used to adorn themselves and were submissive to their husbands, 6 as Sarah obeyed Abraham, calling him lord. And you are now her children if you do right and let nothing terrify you.

7 Likewise you husbands, live considerately with your wives, bestowing honor on the woman as the weaker sex, since you are joint heirs of the grace of life, in order that your prayers may not be hindered.

18.
=====

In Jude 1, we are taught about "Judgment on False Teachers."

5 Now I desire to remind you, though you were once for all fully informed, that he[b] who saved a people out of the land of Egypt, afterward destroyed those who did not believe. 6 And the angels that did not keep their own position but left their proper dwelling have been kept by him in eternal chains in the nether gloom until the judgment of the great day; 7 just as Sodom and Gomor'rah and the surrounding cities,

which likewise acted immorally and indulged in unnatural lust, serve as an example by undergoing a punishment of eternal fire.

8 Yet in like manner these men in their dreamings defile the flesh, reject authority, and revile the glorious ones.[c] 9 But when the archangel Michael, contending with the devil, disputed about the body of Moses, he did not presume to pronounce a reviling judgment upon him, but said, "The Lord rebuke you." 10 But these men revile whatever they do not understand, and by those things that they know by instinct as irrational animals do, they are destroyed. 11 Woe to them! For they walk in the way of Cain, and abandon themselves for the sake of gain to Balaam's error, and perish in Korah's rebellion. 12 These are blemishes[d] on your love feasts, as they boldly carouse together, looking after themselves; waterless clouds, carried along by winds; fruitless trees in late autumn, twice dead, uprooted; 13 wild waves of the sea, casting up the foam of their own shame; wandering stars for whom the nether gloom of darkness has been reserved for ever.

14 It was of these also that Enoch in the seventh generation from Adam prophesied, saying, "Behold, the Lord came with his holy myriads, 15 to execute judgment on all, and to convict all the ungodly of all their deeds of ungodliness which they have committed in such an ungodly way, and of all the harsh things which ungodly sinners have spoken against him." 16 These are grumblers, malcontents,

following their own passions, loud-mouthed boasters, flattering people to gain advantage.

(d) Lessons on Sex from the Revelation to John: Notes

I have decided to not add the passages on sex from the Revelation to John because the book is prophecy about the Apocalypse. It depicts the end times with the completion of God's Divine Plan, and to extract lessons on sex from it would diminish the picture and potency of the prophecy. In God's Divine Plan, the good are rewarded in eternity, while the bad are punished in eternity. With regard to sex, the sexually undefiled and chaste (both men and women) are rewarded, while the sexually immoral and corrupt are punished. The Revelation to John has much to teach us all. As a guide, the lessons on sex include the following 6 passages:

1. In Revelation 14, we are taught about "The Lamb and the 144,000."
2. In Revelation 17, we are taught about "The Great Whore and the Beast."
3. In Revelation 18, we are taught about "The Fall of Babylon."

4. In Revelation 19, we are taught about "The Rejoicing in Heaven."
5. In Revelation 19, we are taught about "The Rider on the White Horse."
6. In Revelation 19, we are taught about "The Beast and Its Armies Defeated."

(4)

POWER

This chapter contains a comprehensive collection of lessons on power from Jesus and the New Testament.

When examining the New Testament, I associated ideas such as might, strength, and authority with power. I do not refer to Jesus' specific miracles that show His power because there are so many examples and because they are supernatural acts of His divinity that are beyond human. Rather, I focus on the moments of power from His exemplary life and the lessons He taught on power.

(a) <u>Lessons on Power from Jesus in the Gospels: 35 Passages</u>

(i) Primary Lessons on Power: 27 Passages

1.
=====

In Matthew 4, "Jesus Ministers to Crowds of People."

23 And he went about all Galilee, teaching in their synagogues and preaching the gospel of the kingdom and healing every disease and every infirmity among the people. 24 So his fame spread throughout all Syria, and they brought him all the sick, those afflicted with various diseases and pains, demoniacs, epileptics, and paralytics, and he healed them. 25 And great crowds followed him from Galilee and the Decap′olis and Jerusalem and Judea and from beyond the Jordan.

2-A.
=====

In Matthew 5, Jesus teaches about "Salt and Light."

13 "You are the salt of the earth; but if salt has lost its taste, how shall its saltness be restored? It is no longer good for anything except to be thrown out and trodden under foot by men.

14 "You are the light of the world. A city set on a hill cannot be hid. 15 Nor do men light a lamp and put it under a bushel, but on a stand, and it gives light to all in the house. 16 Let your light so shine before men, that they may see your good works and give glory to your Father who is in heaven.

2-B.
=====

In Luke 14, Jesus teaches "About Salt."

34 "Salt is good; but if salt has lost its taste, how shall its saltness be restored? 35 It is fit neither for the land nor for the dunghill; men throw it away. He who has ears to hear, let him hear."

3.
=====

In Matthew 9, Jesus teaches that "The Harvest Is Great, the Laborers Few."

35 And Jesus went about all the cities and villages, teaching in their synagogues and preaching the gospel of the kingdom, and healing every disease and every infirmity. 36 When he saw the crowds, he had compassion for them, because they were harassed and helpless, like sheep without a shepherd. 37 Then he said to his disciples, "The harvest is plentiful, but the

laborers are few; 38 pray therefore the Lord of the harvest to send out laborers into his harvest."

4.
=====

In Matthew 10, Jesus assigns "The Mission of the Twelve."

5 These twelve Jesus sent out, charging them, "Go nowhere among the Gentiles, and enter no town of the Samaritans, 6 but go rather to the lost sheep of the house of Israel. 7 And preach as you go, saying, 'The kingdom of heaven is at hand.' 8 Heal the sick, raise the dead, cleanse lepers, cast out demons. You received without paying, give without pay. 9 Take no gold, nor silver, nor copper in your belts, 10 no bag for your journey, nor two tunics, nor sandals, nor a staff; for the laborer deserves his food. 11 And whatever town or village you enter, find out who is worthy in it, and stay with him until you depart. 12 As you enter the house, salute it. 13 And if the house is worthy, let your peace come upon it; but if it is not worthy, let your peace return to you. 14 And if any one will not receive you or listen to your words, shake off the dust from your feet as you leave that house or town. 15 Truly, I say to you, it shall be more tolerable on the day of judgment for the land of Sodom and Gomor'rah than for that town.

5-A.

=====

In Matthew 10, Jesus teaches about "Whom to Fear."

26 "So have no fear of them; for nothing is covered that will not be revealed, or hidden that will not be known. 27 What I tell you in the dark, utter in the light; and what you hear whispered, proclaim upon the housetops. 28 And do not fear those who kill the body but cannot kill the soul; rather fear him who can destroy both soul and body in hell.[d] 29 Are not two sparrows sold for a penny? And not one of them will fall to the ground without your Father's will. 30 But even the hairs of your head are all numbered. 31 Fear not, therefore; you are of more value than many sparrows. 32 So every one who acknowledges me before men, I also will acknowledge before my Father who is in heaven; 33 but whoever denies me before men, I also will deny before my Father who is in heaven.

5-B.

=====

In Luke 12, Jesus teaches about "Exhortation to Fearless Confession."

4 "I tell you, my friends, do not fear those who kill the body, and after that have no more that they can

do. 5 But I will warn you whom to fear: fear him who, after he has killed, has power to cast into hell;[a] yes, I tell you, fear him! 6 Are not five sparrows sold for two pennies? And not one of them is forgotten before God. 7 Why, even the hairs of your head are all numbered. Fear not; you are of more value than many sparrows.

8 "And I tell you, every one who acknowledges me before men, the Son of man also will acknowledge before the angels of God; 9 but he who denies me before men will be denied before the angels of God. 10 And every one who speaks a word against the Son of man will be forgiven; but he who blasphemes against the Holy Spirit will not be forgiven. 11 And when they bring you before the synagogues and the rulers and the authorities, do not be anxious how or what you are to answer or what you are to say; 12 for the Holy Spirit will teach you in that very hour what you ought to say."

6-A.
=====

In Matthew 10, Jesus teaches "Not Peace, but a Sword."

34 "Do not think that I have come to bring peace on earth; I have not come to bring peace, but a sword. 35 For I have come to set a man against his father, and a daughter against her mother, and a daughter-in-law

against her mother-in-law; 36 and a man's foes will be those of his own household. 37 He who loves father or mother more than me is not worthy of me; and he who loves son or daughter more than me is not worthy of me; 38 and he who does not take his cross and follow me is not worthy of me. 39 He who finds his life will lose it, and he who loses his life for my sake will find it.

6-B.
=====

In Luke 12, we learn about "Jesus the Cause of Division."

49 "I came to cast fire upon the earth; and would that it were already kindled! 50 I have a baptism to be baptized with; and how I am constrained until it is accomplished! 51 Do you think that I have come to give peace on earth? No, I tell you, but rather division; 52 for henceforth in one house there will be five divided, three against two and two against three; 53 they will be divided, father against son and son against father, mother against daughter and daughter against her mother, mother-in-law against her daughter-in-law and daughter-in-law against her mother-in-law."

7.

Becoming God-like | JTA

=====

In Matthew 16 (Mark 8, Luke 9), we learn about "Peter's Declaration about Jesus."

13 Now when Jesus came into the district of Caesare'a Philippi, he asked his disciples, "Who do men say that the Son of man is?" 14 And they said, "Some say John the Baptist, others say Eli'jah, and others Jeremiah or one of the prophets." 15 He said to them, "But who do you say that I am?" 16 Simon Peter replied, "You are the Christ, the Son of the living God." 17 And Jesus answered him, "Blessed are you, Simon Bar-Jona! For flesh and blood has not revealed this to you, but my Father who is in heaven. 18 And I tell you, you are Peter,[b] and on this rock[c] I will build my church, and the powers of death[d] shall not prevail against it. 19 I will give you the keys of the kingdom of heaven, and whatever you bind on earth shall be bound in heaven, and whatever you loose on earth shall be loosed in heaven." 20 Then he strictly charged the disciples to tell no one that he was the Christ.

8-A.
=====

In Matthew 17, we learn "Jesus Cures a Boy with a Demon" (Luke 17, "Some Sayings of Jesus").

14 And when they came to the crowd, a man came up to him and kneeling before him said, 15 "Lord, have mercy on my son, for he is an epileptic and he suffers terribly; for often he falls into the fire, and often into the water. 16 And I brought him to your disciples, and they could not heal him." 17 And Jesus answered, "O faithless and perverse generation, how long am I to be with you? How long am I to bear with you? Bring him here to me." 18 And Jesus rebuked him, and the demon came out of him, and the boy was cured instantly. 19 Then the disciples came to Jesus privately and said, "Why could we not cast it out?" 20 He said to them, "Because of your little faith. For truly, I say to you, if you have faith as a grain of mustard seed, you will say to this mountain, 'Move from here to there,' and it will move; and nothing will be impossible to you."[b]

8-B.
=====

In Mark 11 (Matthew 21), Jesus teaches "The Lesson from the Withered Fig Tree."

20 As they passed by in the morning, they saw the fig tree withered away to its roots. 21 And Peter remembered and said to him, "Master,[b] look! The fig tree which you cursed has withered." 22 And Jesus answered them, "Have faith in God. 23 Truly, I say to you, whoever says to this mountain, 'Be taken

up and cast into the sea,' and does not doubt in his heart, but believes that what he says will come to pass, it will be done for him. 24 Therefore I tell you, whatever you ask in prayer, believe that you have received[c] it, and it will be yours. 25 And whenever you stand praying, forgive, if you have anything against any one; so that your Father also who is in heaven may forgive you your trespasses."[d]

9.
=====

In Matthew 21 (Mark 11, Luke 20), we learn about "The Authority of Jesus Questioned."

23 And when he entered the temple, the chief priests and the elders of the people came up to him as he was teaching, and said, "By what authority are you doing these things, and who gave you this authority?" 24 Jesus answered them, "I also will ask you a question; and if you tell me the answer, then I also will tell you by what authority I do these things. 25 The baptism of John, whence was it? From heaven or from men?" And they argued with one another, "If we say, 'From heaven,' he will say to us, 'Why then did you not believe him?' 26 But if we say, 'From men,' we are afraid of the multitude; for all hold that John was a prophet." 27 So they answered Jesus, "We do not know." And he said to them, "Neither will I tell you by what authority I do these things.

10.
=====

In Matthew 24 (Mark 13), Jesus teaches about "The Coming of the Son of Man."

29 "Immediately after the tribulation of those days the sun will be darkened, and the moon will not give its light, and the stars will fall from heaven, and the powers of the heavens will be shaken; 30 then will appear the sign of the Son of man in heaven, and then all the tribes of the earth will mourn, and they will see the Son of man coming on the clouds of heaven with power and great glory; 31 and he will send out his angels with a loud trumpet call, and they will gather his elect from the four winds, from one end of heaven to the other.

11.
=====

In Matthew 25, Jesus teaches about "The Judgment of the Nations."

31 "When the Son of man comes in his glory, and all the angels with him, then he will sit on his glorious throne. 32 Before him will be gathered all the nations, and he will separate them one from another as a shepherd separates the sheep from the goats, 33 and

he will place the sheep at his right hand, but the goats at the left. 34 Then the King will say to those at his right hand, 'Come, O blessed of my Father, inherit the kingdom prepared for you from the foundation of the world; 35 for I was hungry and you gave me food, I was thirsty and you gave me drink, I was a stranger and you welcomed me, 36 I was naked and you clothed me, I was sick and you visited me, I was in prison and you came to me.' 37 Then the righteous will answer him, 'Lord, when did we see thee hungry and feed thee, or thirsty and give thee drink? 38 And when did we see thee a stranger and welcome thee, or naked and clothe thee? 39 And when did we see thee sick or in prison and visit thee?' 40 And the King will answer them, 'Truly, I say to you, as you did it to one of the least of these my brethren, you did it to me.' 41 Then he will say to those at his left hand, 'Depart from me, you cursed, into the eternal fire prepared for the devil and his angels; 42 for I was hungry and you gave me no food, I was thirsty and you gave me no drink, 43 I was a stranger and you did not welcome me, naked and you did not clothe me, sick and in prison and you did not visit me.' 44 Then they also will answer, 'Lord, when did we see thee hungry or thirsty or a stranger or naked or sick or in prison, and did not minister to thee?' 45 Then he will answer them, 'Truly, I say to you, as you did it not to one of the least of these, you did it not to me.' 46 And they will go away into eternal punishment, but the righteous into eternal life."

12-A.
=====

In Mark 3 (Matthew 12), we learn about "Jesus and Beelzebul."

Then he went home; 20 and the crowd came together again, so that they could not even eat. 21 And when his family heard it, they went out to seize him, for people were saying, "He is beside himself." 22 And the scribes who came down from Jerusalem said, "He is possessed by Be-el′zebul, and by the prince of demons he casts out the demons." 23 And he called them to him, and said to them in parables, "How can Satan cast out Satan? 24 If a kingdom is divided against itself, that kingdom cannot stand. 25 And if a house is divided against itself, that house will not be able to stand. 26 And if Satan has risen up against himself and is divided, he cannot stand, but is coming to an end. 27 But no one can enter a strong man's house and plunder his goods, unless he first binds the strong man; then indeed he may plunder his house. 28 "Truly, I say to you, all sins will be forgiven the sons of men, and whatever blasphemies they utter; 29 but whoever blasphemes against the Holy Spirit never has forgiveness, but is guilty of an eternal sin"— 30 for they had said, "He has an unclean spirit."

12-B.

=====

In Luke 11, we learn about "Jesus and Beelzebul."

14 Now he was casting out a demon that was dumb; when the demon had gone out, the dumb man spoke, and the people marveled. 15 But some of them said, "He casts out demons by Be-el'zebul, the prince of demons"; 16 while others, to test him, sought from him a sign from heaven. 17 But he, knowing their thoughts, said to them, "Every kingdom divided against itself is laid waste, and a divided household falls. 18 And if Satan also is divided against himself, how will his kingdom stand? For you say that I cast out demons by Be-el'zebul. 19 And if I cast out demons by Be-el'zebul, by whom do your sons cast them out? Therefore they shall be your judges. 20 But if it is by the finger of God that I cast out demons, then the kingdom of God has come upon you. 21 When a strong man, fully armed, guards his own palace, his goods are in peace; 22 but when one stronger than he assails him and overcomes him, he takes away his armor in which he trusted, and divides his spoil. 23 He who is not with me is against me, and he who does not gather with me scatters.

13.

=====

In Luke 6, "Jesus Teaches and Heals."

17 And he came down with them and stood on a level place, with a great crowd of his disciples and a great multitude of people from all Judea and Jerusalem and the seacoast of Tyre and Sidon, who came to hear him and to be healed of their diseases; 18 and those who were troubled with unclean spirits were cured. 19 And all the crowd sought to touch him, for power came forth from him and healed them all.

14.
=====

In Luke 9 (Mark 6), Jesus assigns "The Mission of the Twelve" (also noted earlier).

9 And he called the twelve together and gave them power and authority over all demons and to cure diseases, 2 and he sent them out to preach the kingdom of God and to heal. 3 And he said to them, "Take nothing for your journey, no staff, nor bag, nor bread, nor money; and do not have two tunics. 4 And whatever house you enter, stay there, and from there depart. 5 And wherever they do not receive you, when you leave that town shake off the dust from your feet as a testimony against them." 6 And they departed and went through the villages, preaching the gospel and healing everywhere.

15.
=====

In Luke 10, Jesus assigns "The Mission of the Seventy."

10 After this the Lord appointed seventy[a] others, and sent them on ahead of him, two by two, into every town and place where he himself was about to come. 2 And he said to them, "The harvest is plentiful, but the laborers are few; pray therefore the Lord of the harvest to send out laborers into his harvest. 3 Go your way; behold, I send you out as lambs in the midst of wolves. 4 Carry no purse, no bag, no sandals; and salute no one on the road. 5 Whatever house you enter, first say, 'Peace be to this house!' 6 And if a son of peace is there, your peace shall rest upon him; but if not, it shall return to you. 7 And remain in the same house, eating and drinking what they provide, for the laborer deserves his wages; do not go from house to house. 8 Whenever you enter a town and they receive you, eat what is set before you; 9 heal the sick in it and say to them, 'The kingdom of God has come near to you.' 10 But whenever you enter a town and they do not receive you, go into its streets and say, 11 'Even the dust of your town that clings to our feet, we wipe off against you; nevertheless know this, that the kingdom of God has come near.' 12 I tell you, it shall be more tolerable on that day for Sodom than for that town.

16.
=====

In Luke 10, we learn about Jesus and "The Return of the Seventy."

17 The seventy[b] returned with joy, saying, "Lord, even the demons are subject to us in your name!" 18 And he said to them, "I saw Satan fall like lightning from heaven. 19 Behold, I have given you authority to tread upon serpents and scorpions, and over all the power of the enemy; and nothing shall hurt you. 20 Nevertheless do not rejoice in this, that the spirits are subject to you; but rejoice that your names are written in heaven."

17.
=====

In Luke 12 (Matthew 24), Jesus teaches about "The Faithful or the Unfaithful Slave."

41 Peter said, "Lord, are you telling this parable for us or for all?" 42 And the Lord said, "Who then is the faithful and wise steward, whom his master will set over his household, to give them their portion of food at the proper time? 43 Blessed is that servant whom his master when he comes will find so doing. 44 Truly, I say to you, he will set him over all his possessions. 45 But if that servant says to himself,

'My master is delayed in coming,' and begins to beat the menservants and the maidservants, and to eat and drink and get drunk, 46 the master of that servant will come on a day when he does not expect him and at an hour he does not know, and will punish[f] him, and put him with the unfaithful. 47 And that servant who knew his master's will, but did not make ready or act according to his will, shall receive a severe beating. 48 But he who did not know, and did what deserved a beating, shall receive a light beating. Every one to whom much is given, of him will much be required; and of him to whom men commit much they will demand the more.

18.
=====

In Luke 18, Jesus teaches "The Parable of the Widow and the Unjust Judge."

18 And he told them a parable, to the effect that they ought always to pray and not lose heart. 2 He said, "In a certain city there was a judge who neither feared God nor regarded man; 3 and there was a widow in that city who kept coming to him and saying, 'Vindicate me against my adversary.' 4 For a while he refused; but afterward he said to himself, 'Though I neither fear God nor regard man, 5 yet because this widow bothers me, I will vindicate her, or she will wear me out by her continual coming.'" 6 And the

Lord said, "Hear what the unrighteous judge says. 7 And will not God vindicate his elect, who cry to him day and night? Will he delay long over them? 8 I tell you, he will vindicate them speedily. Nevertheless, when the Son of man comes, will he find faith on earth?"

19.
=====

In Luke 18, Jesus teaches "The Parable of the Pharisee and the Tax Collector."

9 He also told this parable to some who trusted in themselves that they were righteous and despised others: 10 "Two men went up into the temple to pray, one a Pharisee and the other a tax collector. 11 The Pharisee stood and prayed thus with himself, 'God, I thank thee that I am not like other men, extortioners, unjust, adulterers, or even like this tax collector. 12 I fast twice a week, I give tithes of all that I get.' 13 But the tax collector, standing far off, would not even lift up his eyes to heaven, but beat his breast, saying, 'God, be merciful to me a sinner!' 14 I tell you, this man went down to his house justified rather than the other; for every one who exalts himself will be humbled, but he who humbles himself will be exalted."

20.

=====

In John 8, we learn about "Jesus the Light of the World."

12 Again Jesus spoke to them, saying, "I am the light of the world; he who follows me will not walk in darkness, but will have the light of life." 13 The Pharisees then said to him, "You are bearing witness to yourself; your testimony is not true." 14 Jesus answered, "Even if I do bear witness to myself, my testimony is true, for I know whence I have come and whither I am going, but you do not know whence I come or whither I am going. 15 You judge according to the flesh, I judge no one. 16 Yet even if I do judge, my judgment is true, for it is not I alone that judge, but I and he[b] who sent me. 17 In your law it is written that the testimony of two men is true; 18 I bear witness to myself, and the Father who sent me bears witness to me." 19 They said to him therefore, "Where is your Father?" Jesus answered, "You know neither me nor my Father; if you knew me, you would know my Father also." 20 These words he spoke in the treasury, as he taught in the temple; but no one arrested him, because his hour had not yet come.

21.

=====

In John 8, Jesus teaches about "True Disciples."

31 Jesus then said to the Jews who had believed in him, "If you continue in my word, you are truly my disciples, 32 and you will know the truth, and the truth will make you free." 33 They answered him, "We are descendants of Abraham, and have never been in bondage to any one. How is it that you say, 'You will be made free'?"

34 Jesus answered them, "Truly, truly, I say to you, every one who commits sin is a slave to sin. 35 The slave does not continue in the house for ever; the son continues for ever. 36 So if the Son makes you free, you will be free indeed. 37 I know that you are descendants of Abraham; yet you seek to kill me, because my word finds no place in you. 38 I speak of what I have seen with my Father, and you do what you have heard from your father."

22.
=====

In John 10, we learn about "Jesus the Good Shepherd."

10 "Truly, truly, I say to you, he who does not enter the sheepfold by the door but climbs in by another way, that man is a thief and a robber; 2 but he who enters by the door is the shepherd of the sheep. 3 To him the gatekeeper opens; the sheep hear his voice, and he calls his own sheep by name and leads them

out. 4 When he has brought out all his own, he goes before them, and the sheep follow him, for they know his voice. 5 A stranger they will not follow, but they will flee from him, for they do not know the voice of strangers." 6 This figure Jesus used with them, but they did not understand what he was saying to them. 7 So Jesus again said to them, "Truly, truly, I say to you, I am the door of the sheep. 8 All who came before me are thieves and robbers; but the sheep did not heed them. 9 I am the door; if any one enters by me, he will be saved, and will go in and out and find pasture. 10 The thief comes only to steal and kill and destroy; I came that they may have life, and have it abundantly. 11 I am the good shepherd. The good shepherd lays down his life for the sheep. 12 He who is a hireling and not a shepherd, whose own the sheep are not, sees the wolf coming and leaves the sheep and flees; and the wolf snatches them and scatters them. 13 He flees because he is a hireling and cares nothing for the sheep. 14 I am the good shepherd; I know my own and my own know me, 15 as the Father knows me and I know the Father; and I lay down my life for the sheep. 16 And I have other sheep, that are not of this fold; I must bring them also, and they will heed my voice. So there shall be one flock, one shepherd. 17 For this reason the Father loves me, because I lay down my life, that I may take it again. 18 No one takes it from me, but I lay it down of my own accord. I have power to lay it down, and I have power to take it again; this charge I have received from my Father."

19 There was again a division among the Jews because of these words. 20 Many of them said, "He has a demon, and he is mad; why listen to him?" 21 Others said, "These are not the sayings of one who has a demon. Can a demon open the eyes of the blind?"

23.
=====

In John 14, we learn about "Jesus the Way to the Father."

14 "Let not your hearts be troubled; believe [a] in God, believe also in me. 2 In my Father's house are many rooms; if it were not so, would I have told you that I go to prepare a place for you? 3 And when I go and prepare a place for you, I will come again and will take you to myself, that where I am you may be also. 4 And you know the way where I am going." [b] 5 Thomas said to him, "Lord, we do not know where you are going; how can we know the way?" 6 Jesus said to him, "I am the way, and the truth, and the life; no one comes to the Father, but by me. 7 If you had known me, you would have known my Father also; henceforth you know him and have seen him."
8 Philip said to him, "Lord, show us the Father, and we shall be satisfied." 9 Jesus said to him, "Have I

been with you so long, and yet you do not know me, Philip? He who has seen me has seen the Father; how can you say, 'Show us the Father'? 10 Do you not believe that I am in the Father and the Father in me? The words that I say to you I do not speak on my own authority; but the Father who dwells in me does his works. 11 Believe me that I am in the Father and the Father in me; or else believe me for the sake of the works themselves.

12 "Truly, truly, I say to you, he who believes in me will also do the works that I do; and greater works than these will he do, because I go to the Father. 13 Whatever you ask in my name, I will do it, that the Father may be glorified in the Son; 14 if you ask[c] anything in my name, I will do it.

24.
=====

In John 14, Jesus announces "The Promise of the Holy Spirit."

15 "If you love me, you will keep my commandments. 16 And I will pray the Father, and he will give you another Counselor, to be with you for ever, 17 even the Spirit of truth, whom the world cannot receive, because it neither sees him nor knows him; you know him, for he dwells with you, and will be in you.

18 "I will not leave you desolate; I will come to you. 19 Yet a little while, and the world will see me no more, but you will see me; because I live, you will live also. 20 In that day you will know that I am in my Father, and you in me, and I in you. 21 He who has my commandments and keeps them, he it is who loves me; and he who loves me will be loved by my Father, and I will love him and manifest myself to him." 22 Judas (not Iscariot) said to him, "Lord, how is it that you will manifest yourself to us, and not to the world?" 23 Jesus answered him, "If a man loves me, he will keep my word, and my Father will love him, and we will come to him and make our home with him. 24 He who does not love me does not keep my words; and the word which you hear is not mine but the Father's who sent me.

25 "These things I have spoken to you, while I am still with you. 26 But the Counselor, the Holy Spirit, whom the Father will send in my name, he will teach you all things, and bring to your remembrance all that I have said to you. 27 Peace I leave with you; my peace I give to you; not as the world gives do I give to you. Let not your hearts be troubled, neither let them be afraid. 28 You heard me say to you, 'I go away, and I will come to you.' If you loved me, you would have rejoiced, because I go to the Father; for the Father is greater than I. 29 And now I have told you before it takes place, so that when it does take place, you may believe. 30 I will no longer talk much with you, for the ruler of this world is coming. He has

no power over me; 31 but I do as the Father has commanded me, so that the world may know that I love the Father. Rise, let us go hence.

25.
=====

In John 15, we learn about "Jesus the True Vine."

15 "I am the true vine, and my Father is the vinedresser. 2 Every branch of mine that bears no fruit, he takes away, and every branch that does bear fruit he prunes, that it may bear more fruit. 3 You are already made clean by the word which I have spoken to you. 4 Abide in me, and I in you. As the branch cannot bear fruit by itself, unless it abides in the vine, neither can you, unless you abide in me. 5 I am the vine, you are the branches. He who abides in me, and I in him, he it is that bears much fruit, for apart from me you can do nothing. 6 If a man does not abide in me, he is cast forth as a branch and withers; and the branches are gathered, thrown into the fire and burned. 7 If you abide in me, and my words abide in you, ask whatever you will, and it shall be done for you. 8 By this my Father is glorified, that you bear much fruit, and so prove to be my disciples. 9 As the Father has loved me, so have I loved you; abide in my love. 10 If you keep my commandments, you will abide in my love, just as I have kept my Father's commandments and abide in his love. 11 These things

I have spoken to you, that my joy may be in you, and that your joy may be full.

12 "This is my commandment, that you love one another as I have loved you. 13 Greater love has no man than this, that a man lay down his life for his friends. 14 You are my friends if you do what I command you. 15 No longer do I call you servants,[a] for the servant[b] does not know what his master is doing; but I have called you friends, for all that I have heard from my Father I have made known to you. 16 You did not choose me, but I chose you and appointed you that you should go and bear fruit and that your fruit should abide; so that whatever you ask the Father in my name, he may give it to you. 17 This I command you, to love one another.

26.

=====

In John 16, Jesus teaches about "The Work of the Spirit."

"I did not say these things to you from the beginning, because I was with you. 5 But now I am going to him who sent me; yet none of you asks me, 'Where are you going?' 6 But because I have said these things to you, sorrow has filled your hearts. 7 Nevertheless I tell you the truth: it is to your advantage that I go away, for if I do not go away, the Counselor will not come to you; but if I go, I will send him to you. 8 And when he comes, he will convince[a] the world concerning sin and righteousness and judgment: 9 concerning sin, because they do not believe in me; 10 concerning righteousness, because I go to the Father, and you will see me no more; 11 concerning judgment, because the ruler of this world is judged. 12 "I have yet many things to say to you, but you cannot bear them now. 13 When the Spirit of truth comes, he will guide you into all the truth; for he will not speak on his own authority, but whatever he hears he will speak, and he will declare to you the things that are to come. 14 He will glorify me, for he will take what is mine and declare it to you. 15 All that the Father has is mine; therefore I said that he will take what is mine and declare it to you.

27.
=====

In John 17, "Jesus Prays for His Disciples."

17 When Jesus had spoken these words, he lifted up his eyes to heaven and said, "Father, the hour has come; glorify thy Son that the Son may glorify thee, 2 since thou hast given him power over all flesh, to give eternal life to all whom thou hast given him. 3 And this is eternal life, that they know thee the only true God, and Jesus Christ whom thou hast sent. 4 I glorified thee on earth, having accomplished the work which thou gavest me to do; 5 and now, Father,

Becoming God-like | JTA

glorify thou me in thy own presence with the glory which I had with thee before the world was made. 6 "I have manifested thy name to the men whom thou gavest me out of the world; thine they were, and thou gavest them to me, and they have kept thy word. 7 Now they know that everything that thou hast given me is from thee; 8 for I have given them the words which thou gavest me, and they have received them and know in truth that I came from thee; and they have believed that thou didst send me. 9 I am praying for them; I am not praying for the world but for those whom thou hast given me, for they are thine; 10 all mine are thine, and thine are mine, and I am glorified in them. 11 And now I am no more in the world, but they are in the world, and I am coming to thee. Holy Father, keep them in thy name, which thou hast given me, that they may be one, even as we are one. 12 While I was with them, I kept them in thy name, which thou hast given me; I have guarded them, and none of them is lost but the son of perdition, that the scripture might be fulfilled. 13 But now I am coming to thee; and these things I speak in the world, that they may have my joy fulfilled in themselves. 14 I have given them thy word; and the world has hated them because they are not of the world, even as I am not of the world. 15 I do not pray that thou shouldst take them out of the world, but that thou shouldst keep them from the evil one.[a] 16 They are not of the world, even as I am not of the world. 17 Sanctify them in the truth; thy word is truth. 18 As thou didst send me into the world, so I have sent them into the world. 19 And for their sake I consecrate myself, that they also may be consecrated in truth.

20 "I do not pray for these only, but also for those who believe in me through their word, 21 that they may all be one; even as thou, Father, art in me, and I in thee, that they also may be in us, so that the world may believe that thou hast sent me. 22 The glory which thou hast given me I have given to them, that they may be one even as we are one, 23 I in them and thou in me, that they may become perfectly one, so that the world may know that thou hast sent me and hast loved them even as thou hast loved me. 24 Father, I desire that they also, whom thou hast given me, may be with me where I am, to behold my glory which thou hast given me in thy love for me before the foundation of the world. 25 O righteous Father, the world has not known thee, but I have known thee; and these know that thou hast sent me. 26 I made known to them thy name, and I will make it known, that the love with which thou hast loved me may be in them, and I in them."

(ii) Supporting Lessons on Power: 8 Passages

1.

=====

In Matthew 4 (Mark 1, Luke 4), we learn about "The Temptation of Jesus."

4 Then Jesus was led up by the Spirit into the wilderness to be tempted by the devil. 2 And he fasted forty days and forty nights, and afterward he was hungry. 3 And the tempter came and said to him, "If you are the Son of God, command these stones to become loaves of bread." 4 But he answered, "It is written,
'Man shall not live by bread alone,
but by every word that proceeds from the mouth of God.'"
5 Then the devil took him to the holy city, and set him on the pinnacle of the temple, 6 and said to him, "If you are the Son of God, throw yourself down; for it is written,
'He will give his angels charge of you,'
and
'On their hands they will bear you up,
lest you strike your foot against a stone.'"
7 Jesus said to him, "Again it is written, 'You shall not tempt the Lord your God.'" 8 Again, the devil took him to a very high mountain, and showed him all the kingdoms of the world and the glory of them; 9 and he said to him, "All these I will give you, if you will fall down and worship me." 10 Then Jesus said to him, "Begone, Satan! for it is written,
'You shall worship the Lord your God

and him only shall you serve.'"

11 Then the devil left him, and behold, angels came and ministered to him.

2.
=====

In Matthew 7, Jesus teaches about "Ask, Search, Knock."

7 "Ask, and it will be given you; seek, and you will find; knock, and it will be opened to you. 8 For every one who asks receives, and he who seeks finds, and to him who knocks it will be opened. 9 Or what man of you, if his son asks him for bread, will give him a stone? 10 Or if he asks for a fish, will give him a serpent? 11 If you then, who are evil, know how to give good gifts to your children, how much more will your Father who is in heaven give good things to those who ask him!

3.
=====

In Matthew 7, Jesus teaches "The Golden Rule."

12 So whatever you wish that men would do to you, do so to them; for this is the law and the prophets.

4.

=====

In Matthew 7 (Luke 6), Jesus teaches about "Hearers and Doers."

24 "Every one then who hears these words of mine and does them will be like a wise man who built his house upon the rock; 25 and the rain fell, and the floods came, and the winds blew and beat upon that house, but it did not fall, because it had been founded on the rock. 26 And every one who hears these words of mine and does not do them will be like a foolish man who built his house upon the sand; 27 and the rain fell, and the floods came, and the winds blew and beat against that house, and it fell; and great was the fall of it."
28 And when Jesus finished these sayings, the crowds were astonished at his teaching, 29 for he taught them as one who had authority, and not as their scribes.

5.

=====

In Matthew 27 (Mark 15), we learn "Pilate Questions Jesus."

11 Now Jesus stood before the governor; and the governor asked him, "Are you the King of the Jews?" Jesus said, "You have said so." 12 But when he was accused by the chief priests and elders, he made no

answer. 13 Then Pilate said to him, "Do you not hear how many things they testify against you?" 14 But he gave him no answer, not even to a single charge; so that the governor wondered greatly.

6.
=====

In Luke 11, Jesus teaches about "Perseverance in Prayer."

5 And he said to them, "Which of you who has a friend will go to him at midnight and say to him, 'Friend, lend me three loaves; 6 for a friend of mine has arrived on a journey, and I have nothing to set before him'; 7 and he will answer from within, 'Do not bother me; the door is now shut, and my children are with me in bed; I cannot get up and give you anything'? 8 I tell you, though he will not get up and give him anything because he is his friend, yet because of his importunity he will rise and give him whatever he needs. 9 And I tell you, Ask, and it will be given you; seek, and you will find; knock, and it will be opened to you. 10 For every one who asks receives, and he who seeks finds, and to him who knocks it will be opened. 11 What father among you, if his son asks for[b] a fish, will instead of a fish give him a serpent; 12 or if he asks for an egg, will give him a scorpion? 13 If you then, who are evil, know how to give good gifts to your children, how much

more will the heavenly Father give the Holy Spirit to those who ask him!"

7.
=====

In Luke 11, Jesus teaches about "The Light of the Body."

33 "No one after lighting a lamp puts it in a cellar or under a bushel, but on a stand, that those who enter may see the light. 34 Your eye is the lamp of your body; when your eye is sound, your whole body is full of light; but when it is not sound, your body is full of darkness. 35 Therefore be careful lest the light in you be darkness. 36 If then your whole body is full of light, having no part dark, it will be wholly bright, as when a lamp with its rays gives you light."

8.
=====

In John 16, Jesus teaches about "Peace for the Disciples."

25 "I have said this to you in figures; the hour is coming when I shall no longer speak to you in figures but tell you plainly of the Father. 26 In that day you will ask in my name; and I do not say to you that I shall pray the Father for you; 27 for the Father

himself loves you, because you have loved me and have believed that I came from the Father. 28 I came from the Father and have come into the world; again, I am leaving the world and going to the Father."
29 His disciples said, "Ah, now you are speaking plainly, not in any figure! 30 Now we know that you know all things, and need none to question you; by this we believe that you came from God." 31 Jesus answered them, "Do you now believe? 32 The hour is coming, indeed it has come, when you will be scattered, every man to his home, and will leave me alone; yet I am not alone, for the Father is with me. 33 I have said this to you, that in me you may have peace. In the world you have tribulation; but be of good cheer, I have overcome the world."

(b) <u>Lessons on Power from the Acts of the Apostles: Notes</u>

The book known as the Acts of the Apostles is filled with acts of power. The book is the history of the early Church and the Apostles' mighty deeds, which include ministry, traveling, teaching, preaching, and miracles. The Apostles are described as heroes filled with the Holy Spirit on a mission to spread the good news of Jesus Christ. I have not cited lessons on power from this book because it is filled with acts of power, and it should be read directly by those who are interested in learning more about power as defined by the early Christian movement.

(c) **Lessons on Power from the Letters: 5 Passages**

These letters are mostly by Saint Paul, who is known as the Apostle to the Gentiles.

1.
=====

In 2 Thessalonians 2, Paul teaches about "The Man of Lawlessness."

2 Now concerning the coming of our Lord Jesus Christ and our assembling to meet him, we beg you, brethren, 2 not to be quickly shaken in mind or excited, either by spirit or by word, or by letter purporting to be from us, to the effect that the day of the Lord has come. 3 Let no one deceive you in any way; for that day will not come, unless the rebellion comes first, and the man of lawlessness[a] is revealed, the son of perdition, 4 who opposes and exalts

himself against every so-called god or object of worship, so that he takes his seat in the temple of God, proclaiming himself to be God. 5 Do you not remember that when I was still with you I told you this? 6 And you know what is restraining him now so that he may be revealed in his time. 7 For the mystery of lawlessness is already at work; only he who now restrains it will do so until he is out of the way. 8 And then the lawless one will be revealed, and the Lord Jesus will slay him with the breath of his mouth and destroy him by his appearing and his coming. 9 The coming of the lawless one by the activity of Satan will be with all power and with pretended signs and wonders, 10 and with all wicked deception for those who are to perish, because they refused to love the truth and so be saved. 11 Therefore God sends upon them a strong delusion, to make them believe what is false, 12 so that all may be condemned who did not believe the truth but had pleasure in unrighteousness.

2.
=====

In 2 Peter 2, we learn about "False Prophets and Their Punishment."

2 But false prophets also arose among the people, just as there will be false teachers among you, who will secretly bring in destructive heresies, even denying the Master who bought them, bringing upon

themselves swift destruction. 2 And many will follow their licentiousness, and because of them the way of truth will be reviled. 3 And in their greed they will exploit you with false words; from of old their condemnation has not been idle, and their destruction has not been asleep.

4 For if God did not spare the angels when they sinned, but cast them into hell[a] and committed them to pits of nether gloom to be kept until the judgment; 5 if he did not spare the ancient world, but preserved Noah, a herald of righteousness, with seven other persons, when he brought a flood upon the world of the ungodly; 6 if by turning the cities of Sodom and Gomor'rah to ashes he condemned them to extinction and made them an example to those who were to be ungodly; 7 and if he rescued righteous Lot, greatly distressed by the licentiousness of the wicked 8 (for by what that righteous man saw and heard as he lived among them, he was vexed in his righteous soul day after day with their lawless deeds), 9 then the Lord knows how to rescue the godly from trial, and to keep the unrighteous under punishment until the day of judgment, 10 and especially those who indulge in the lust of defiling passion and despise authority.

Bold and wilful, they are not afraid to revile the glorious ones, 11 whereas angels, though greater in might and power, do not pronounce a reviling judgment upon them before the Lord. 12 But these, like irrational animals, creatures of instinct, born to be caught and killed, reviling in matters of which they are ignorant, will be destroyed in the same destruction with them, 13 suffering wrong for their wrongdoing. They count it pleasure to revel in the daytime. They are blots and blemishes, reveling in their dissipation,[b] carousing with you. 14 They have eyes full of adultery, insatiable for sin. They entice unsteady souls. They have hearts trained in greed. Accursed children! 15 Forsaking the right way they have gone astray; they have followed the way of Balaam, the son of Be'or, who loved gain from wrongdoing, 16 but was rebuked for his own transgression; a dumb ass spoke with human voice and restrained the prophet's madness.

17 These are waterless springs and mists driven by a storm; for them the nether gloom of darkness has been reserved. 18 For, uttering loud boasts of folly, they entice with licentious passions of the flesh men who have barely escaped from those who live in error. 19 They promise them freedom, but they themselves are slaves of corruption; for whatever overcomes a man, to that he is enslaved. 20 For if, after they have escaped the defilements of the world through the knowledge of our Lord and Savior Jesus Christ, they are again entangled in them and overpowered, the last state has become worse for them than the first. 21 For it would have been better for them never to have known the way of righteousness than after knowing it to turn back from the holy commandment delivered to them. 22 It has happened to them according to the true proverb, The

dog turns back to his own vomit, and the sow is washed only to wallow in the mire.

3.
=====

In 1 John 5, we learn "Faith Conquers the World."

5 Every one who believes that Jesus is the Christ is a child of God, and every one who loves the parent loves the child. 2 By this we know that we love the children of God, when we love God and obey his commandments. 3 For this is the love of God, that we keep his commandments. And his commandments are not burdensome. 4 For whatever is born of God overcomes the world; and this is the victory that overcomes the world, our faith. 5 Who is it that overcomes the world but he who believes that Jesus is the Son of God?

4.
=====

In 1 John 5, we learn about "Testimony concerning the Son of God."

6 This is he who came by water and blood, Jesus Christ, not with the water only but with the water and the blood. 7 And the Spirit is the witness, because the Spirit is the truth. 8 There are three witnesses, the

Spirit, the water, and the blood; and these three agree. 9 If we receive the testimony of men, the testimony of God is greater; for this is the testimony of God that he has borne witness to his Son. 10 He who believes in the Son of God has the testimony in himself. He who does not believe God has made him a liar, because he has not believed in the testimony that God has borne to his Son. 11 And this is the testimony, that God gave us eternal life, and this life is in his Son. 12 He who has the Son has life; he who has not the Son of God has not life.

5.
======

In Jude, we learn about "Judgment on False Teachers."

5 Now I desire to remind you, though you were once for all fully informed, that he[b] who saved a people out of the land of Egypt, afterward destroyed those who did not believe. 6 And the angels that did not keep their own position but left their proper dwelling have been kept by him in eternal chains in the nether gloom until the judgment of the great day; 7 just as Sodom and Gomor'rah and the surrounding cities, which likewise acted immorally and indulged in unnatural lust, serve as an example by undergoing a punishment of eternal fire.

8 Yet in like manner these men in their dreamings defile the flesh, reject authority, and revile the glorious ones.[c] 9 But when the archangel Michael, contending with the devil, disputed about the body of Moses, he did not presume to pronounce a reviling judgment upon him, but said, "The Lord rebuke you." 10 But these men revile whatever they do not understand, and by those things that they know by instinct as irrational animals do, they are destroyed. 11 Woe to them! For they walk in the way of Cain, and abandon themselves for the sake of gain to Balaam's error, and perish in Korah's rebellion. 12 These are blemishes[d] on your love feasts, as they boldly carouse together, looking after themselves; waterless clouds, carried along by winds; fruitless trees in late autumn, twice dead, uprooted; 13 wild waves of the sea, casting up the foam of their own shame; wandering stars for whom the nether gloom of darkness has been reserved for ever.

14 It was of these also that Enoch in the seventh generation from Adam prophesied, saying, "Behold, the Lord came with his holy myriads, 15 to execute judgment on all, and to convict all the ungodly of all their deeds of ungodliness which they have committed in such an ungodly way, and of all the harsh things which ungodly sinners have spoken against him." 16 These are grumblers, malcontents, following their own passions, loud-mouthed boasters, flattering people to gain advantage.

(d) Lessons on Power from the Revelation to John: Notes

I have not cited lessons on power from the Revelation to John because the book is Apocalyptic Prophecy that is filled with powerful images depicting the end times with the completion of God's Divine Plan. Angels and demons go to war in a battle of good versus evil with God's elect destined for victory. Redemption is awarded to the good, and God and His Son are enthroned over a new heaven and a new earth. To extract lessons on power from the Revelation to John would diminish the picture and potency of the prophecy. The entire book is filled with powerful moments that we can learn from.

(5)

FAME

This chapter contains a comprehensive collection of lessons on fame from Jesus and the New Testament.

I have cited in full the primary and supporting lessons on fame from Jesus in the Gospels. There are many lessons, so for the sake of brevity without neglect, I have simply listed the lessons on fame that remain in the New Testament from the Acts of the Apostles, the Letters, and the Revelation to John.

(a) Lessons on Fame from Jesus in the Gospels: 45 Passages

(i) Primary Lessons on Fame: 36 Passages

1.
=====

In Matthew 4, "Jesus Ministers to Crowds of People."

23 And he went about all Galilee, teaching in their synagogues and preaching the gospel of the kingdom and healing every disease and every infirmity among the people. 24 So his fame spread throughout all Syria, and they brought him all the sick, those afflicted with various diseases and pains, demoniacs, epileptics, and paralytics, and he healed them. 25 And great crowds followed him from Galilee and the Decap′olis and Jerusalem and Judea and from beyond the Jordan.

2-A.
=====

In Matthew 5, Jesus teaches about "Salt and Light."

13 "You are the salt of the earth; but if salt has lost its taste, how shall its saltness be restored? It is no longer good for anything except to be thrown out and trodden under foot by men.
14 "You are the light of the world. A city set on a hill cannot be hid. 15 Nor do men light a lamp and put it under a bushel, but on a stand, and it gives light to all

in the house. 16 Let your light so shine before men, that they may see your good works and give glory to your Father who is in heaven.

2-B.
=====

In Mark 4, Jesus teaches about "A Lamp under a Bushel Basket."

21 And he said to them, "Is a lamp brought in to be put under a bushel, or under a bed, and not on a stand? 22 For there is nothing hid, except to be made manifest; nor is anything secret, except to come to light. 23 If any man has ears to hear, let him hear." 24 And he said to them, "Take heed what you hear; the measure you give will be the measure you get, and still more will be given you. 25 For to him who has will more be given; and from him who has not, even what he has will be taken away."

2-C.
=====

In Luke 8, Jesus teaches about "A Lamp under a Jar."

16 "No one after lighting a lamp covers it with a vessel, or puts it under a bed, but puts it on a stand, that those who enter may see the light. 17 For nothing is hid that shall not be made manifest, nor anything

secret that shall not be known and come to light. 18 Take heed then how you hear; for to him who has will more be given, and from him who has not, even what he thinks that he has will be taken away."

3.
=====

In Matthew 6, Jesus teaches "Concerning Almsgiving."

6 "Beware of practicing your piety before men in order to be seen by them; for then you will have no reward from your Father who is in heaven.
2 "Thus, when you give alms, sound no trumpet before you, as the hypocrites do in the synagogues and in the streets, that they may be praised by men. Truly, I say to you, they have received their reward. 3 But when you give alms, do not let your left hand know what your right hand is doing, 4 so that your alms may be in secret; and your Father who sees in secret will reward you.

4.
=====

In Matthew 6 (Luke 11), Jesus teaches "Concerning Prayer."

5 "And when you pray, you must not be like the hypocrites; for they love to stand and pray in the synagogues and at the street corners, that they may be seen by men. Truly, I say to you, they have received their reward. 6 But when you pray, go into your room and shut the door and pray to your Father who is in secret; and your Father who sees in secret will reward you.

7 "And in praying do not heap up empty phrases as the Gentiles do; for they think that they will be heard for their many words. 8 Do not be like them, for your Father knows what you need before you ask him. 9 Pray then like this:

Our Father who art in heaven,

Hallowed be thy name.

10 Thy kingdom come,

Thy will be done,

   On earth as it is in heaven.

11 Give us this day our daily bread;[a]

12 And forgive us our debts,

   As we also have forgiven our debtors;

13 And lead us not into temptation,

   But deliver us from evil.[b]

14 For if you forgive men their trespasses, your heavenly Father also will forgive you; 15 but if you do not forgive men their trespasses, neither will your Father forgive your trespasses.

5.

=====

In Matthew 6, Jesus teaches "Concerning Fasting."

16 "And when you fast, do not look dismal, like the hypocrites, for they disfigure their faces that their fasting may be seen by men. Truly, I say to you, they have received their reward. 17 But when you fast, anoint your head and wash your face, 18 that your fasting may not be seen by men but by your Father who is in secret; and your Father who sees in secret will reward you.

6-A.

=====

In Matthew 7, Jesus teaches about "A Tree and Its Fruit."

15 "Beware of false prophets, who come to you in sheep's clothing but inwardly are ravenous wolves. 16 You will know them by their fruits. Are grapes gathered from thorns, or figs from thistles? 17 So, every sound tree bears good fruit, but the bad tree bears evil fruit. 18 A sound tree cannot bear evil fruit, nor can a bad tree bear good fruit. 19 Every tree that does not bear good fruit is cut down and thrown into the fire. 20 Thus you will know them by their fruits.

6-B.

=====

In Matthew 12, Jesus teaches about "A Tree and Its Fruit."

33 "Either make the tree good, and its fruit good; or make the tree bad, and its fruit bad; for the tree is known by its fruit. 34 You brood of vipers! how can you speak good, when you are evil? For out of the abundance of the heart the mouth speaks. 35 The good man out of his good treasure brings forth good, and the evil man out of his evil treasure brings forth evil. 36 I tell you, on the day of judgment men will render account for every careless word they utter; 37 for by your words you will be justified, and by your words you will be condemned."

6-C.

=====

In Luke 6, Jesus teaches about "A Tree and Its Fruit."

43 "For no good tree bears bad fruit, nor again does a bad tree bear good fruit; 44 for each tree is known by its own fruit. For figs are not gathered from thorns, nor are grapes picked from a bramble bush. 45 The good man out of the good treasure of his heart produces good, and the evil man out of his evil treasure produces evil; for out of the abundance of the heart his mouth speaks.

7.
=====

In Matthew 7, Jesus teaches "Concerning Self-Deception."

21 "Not every one who says to me, 'Lord, Lord,' shall enter the kingdom of heaven, but he who does the will of my Father who is in heaven. 22 On that day many will say to me, 'Lord, Lord, did we not prophesy in your name, and cast out demons in your name, and do many mighty works in your name?' 23 And then will I declare to them, 'I never knew you; depart from me, you evildoers.'

8-A.
=====

In Matthew 10, Jesus teaches about "Whom to Fear."

26 "So have no fear of them; for nothing is covered that will not be revealed, or hidden that will not be known. 27 What I tell you in the dark, utter in the light; and what you hear whispered, proclaim upon the housetops. 28 And do not fear those who kill the body but cannot kill the soul; rather fear him who can destroy both soul and body in hell.[d] 29 Are not two sparrows sold for a penny? And not one of them will fall to the ground without your Father's will. 30 But even the hairs of your head are all numbered. 31 Fear

not, therefore; you are of more value than many sparrows. 32 So every one who acknowledges me before men, I also will acknowledge before my Father who is in heaven; 33 but whoever denies me before men, I also will deny before my Father who is in heaven.

8-B.
=====

In Luke 12, Jesus teaches about "Exhortation to Fearless Confession."

4 "I tell you, my friends, do not fear those who kill the body, and after that have no more that they can do. 5 But I will warn you whom to fear: fear him who, after he has killed, has power to cast into hell;[a] yes, I tell you, fear him! 6 Are not five sparrows sold for two pennies? And not one of them is forgotten before God. 7 Why, even the hairs of your head are all numbered. Fear not; you are of more value than many sparrows.
8 "And I tell you, every one who acknowledges me before men, the Son of man also will acknowledge before the angels of God; 9 but he who denies me before men will be denied before the angels of God. 10 And every one who speaks a word against the Son of man will be forgiven; but he who blasphemes against the Holy Spirit will not be forgiven. 11 And when they bring you before the synagogues and the

rulers and the authorities, do not be anxious how or what you are to answer or what you are to say; 12 for the Holy Spirit will teach you in that very hour what you ought to say."

9.
=====

In Matthew 12, we learn about "God's Chosen Servant."

15 Jesus, aware of this, withdrew from there. And many followed him, and he healed them all, 16 and ordered them not to make him known. 17 This was to fulfil what was spoken by the prophet Isaiah:
18 "Behold, my servant whom I have chosen,
  my beloved with whom my soul is well pleased.
I will put my Spirit upon him,
  and he shall proclaim justice to the Gentiles.
19 He will not wrangle or cry aloud,
  nor will any one hear his voice in the streets;
20 he will not break a bruised reed
  or quench a smoldering wick,
till he brings justice to victory;
21   and in his name will the Gentiles hope."

10.
=====

In Matthew 13 (Mark 6, Luke 4), we learn about "The Rejection of Jesus at Nazareth."

53 And when Jesus had finished these parables, he went away from there, 54 and coming to his own country he taught them in their synagogue, so that they were astonished, and said, "Where did this man get this wisdom and these mighty works? 55 Is not this the carpenter's son? Is not his mother called Mary? And are not his brothers James and Joseph and Simon and Judas? 56 And are not all his sisters with us? Where then did this man get all this?" 57 And they took offense at him. But Jesus said to them, "A prophet is not without honor except in his own country and in his own house." 58 And he did not do many mighty works there, because of their unbelief.

11.
=====

In Matthew 16 (Mark 8), Jesus teaches about "The Yeast of the Pharisees and Sadducees."

5 When the disciples reached the other side, they had forgotten to bring any bread. 6 Jesus said to them, "Take heed and beware of the leaven of the Pharisees and Sad'ducees." 7 And they discussed it among themselves, saying, "We brought no bread." 8 But Jesus, aware of this, said, "O men of little faith, why do you discuss among yourselves the fact that you

have no bread? 9 Do you not yet perceive? Do you not remember the five loaves of the five thousand, and how many baskets you gathered? 10 Or the seven loaves of the four thousand, and how many baskets you gathered? 11 How is it that you fail to perceive that I did not speak about bread? Beware of the leaven of the Pharisees and Sad'ducees." 12 Then they understood that he did not tell them to beware of the leaven of bread, but of the teaching of the Pharisees and Sad'ducees.

12.
=====

In Matthew 16 (Mark 8, Luke 9), we learn about "Peter's Declaration about Jesus."

13 Now when Jesus came into the district of Caesare'a Philippi, he asked his disciples, "Who do men say that the Son of man is?" 14 And they said, "Some say John the Baptist, others say Eli'jah, and others Jeremiah or one of the prophets." 15 He said to them, "But who do you say that I am?" 16 Simon Peter replied, "You are the Christ, the Son of the living God." 17 And Jesus answered him, "Blessed are you, Simon Bar-Jona! For flesh and blood has not revealed this to you, but my Father who is in heaven. 18 And I tell you, you are Peter,[b] and on this rock[c] I will build my church, and the powers of death[d] shall not prevail against it. 19 I will give you

the keys of the kingdom of heaven, and whatever you bind on earth shall be bound in heaven, and whatever you loose on earth shall be loosed in heaven." 20 Then he strictly charged the disciples to tell no one that he was the Christ.

13.
=====

In Matthew 16 (Luke 9), Jesus teaches about "The Cross and Self-Denial."

24 Then Jesus told his disciples, "If any man would come after me, let him deny himself and take up his cross and follow me. 25 For whoever would save his life will lose it, and whoever loses his life for my sake will find it. 26 For what will it profit a man, if he gains the whole world and forfeits his life? Or what shall a man give in return for his life? 27 For the Son of man is to come with his angels in the glory of his Father, and then he will repay every man for what he has done. 28 Truly, I say to you, there are some standing here who will not taste death before they see the Son of man coming in his kingdom."

14.
=====

In Matthew 24 (Mark 13, Luke 21), Jesus teaches "The Lesson of the Fig Tree."

32 "From the fig tree learn its lesson: as soon as its branch becomes tender and puts forth its leaves, you know that summer is near. 33 So also, when you see all these things, you know that he is near, at the very gates. 34 Truly, I say to you, this generation will not pass away till all these things take place. 35 Heaven and earth will pass away, but my words will not pass away.

15.
=====
In Mark 1, Jesus gives "A Preaching Tour in Galilee."

35 And in the morning, a great while before day, he rose and went out to a lonely place, and there he prayed. 36 And Simon and those who were with him pursued him, 37 and they found him and said to him, "Every one is searching for you." 38 And he said to them, "Let us go on to the next towns, that I may preach there also; for that is why I came out." 39 And he went throughout all Galilee, preaching in their synagogues and casting out demons.

16.
=====
In Mark 12 (Luke 20), "Jesus Denounces the Scribes."

38 And in his teaching he said, "Beware of the scribes, who like to go about in long robes, and to have salutations in the market places 39 and the best seats in the synagogues and the places of honor at feasts, 40 who devour widows' houses and for a pretense make long prayers. They will receive the greater condemnation."

17.
=====

In Mark 13 (Matthew 24), Jesus teaches about "Persecution Foretold."

9 "But take heed to yourselves; for they will deliver you up to councils; and you will be beaten in synagogues; and you will stand before governors and kings for my sake, to bear testimony before them. 10 And the gospel must first be preached to all nations. 11 And when they bring you to trial and deliver you up, do not be anxious beforehand what you are to say; but say whatever is given you in that hour, for it is not you who speak, but the Holy Spirit. 12 And brother will deliver up brother to death, and the father his child, and children will rise against parents and have them put to death; 13 and you will be hated by all for my name's sake. But he who endures to the end will be saved.

18.
=====

In Luke 4 (Matthew 4, Mark 1), we learn about Jesus and "The Beginning of the Galilean Ministry."

14 And Jesus returned in the power of the Spirit into Galilee, and a report concerning him went out through all the surrounding country. 15 And he taught in their synagogues, being glorified by all.

19.
=====

In Luke 4, "Jesus Preaches in the Synagogues."

42 And when it was day he departed and went into a lonely place. And the people sought him and came to him, and would have kept him from leaving them; 43 but he said to them, "I must preach the good news of the kingdom of God to the other cities also; for I was sent for this purpose." 44 And he was preaching in the synagogues of Judea.[b]

20.
=====

In Luke 6, "Jesus Teaches and Heals."

17 And he came down with them and stood on a level place, with a great crowd of his disciples and a great multitude of people from all Judea and Jerusalem and the seacoast of Tyre and Sidon, who came to hear him and to be healed of their diseases; 18 and those who were troubled with unclean spirits were cured. 19 And all the crowd sought to touch him, for power came forth from him and healed them all.

21.
=====

In Luke 7 (Matthew 11), Jesus speaks with "Messengers from John the Baptist."

18 The disciples of John told him of all these things. 19 And John, calling to him two of his disciples, sent them to the Lord, saying, "Are you he who is to come, or shall we look for another?" 20 And when the men had come to him, they said, "John the Baptist has sent us to you, saying, 'Are you he who is to come, or shall we look for another?'" 21 In that hour he cured many of diseases and plagues and evil spirits, and on many that were blind he bestowed sight. 22 And he answered them, "Go and tell John what you have seen and heard: the blind receive their sight, the lame walk, lepers are cleansed, and the deaf hear, the dead are raised up, the poor have good news preached to them. 23 And blessed is he who takes no offense at me."

24 When the messengers of John had gone, he began to speak to the crowds concerning John: "What did you go out into the wilderness to behold? A reed shaken by the wind? 25 What then did you go out to see? A man clothed in soft clothing? Behold, those who are gorgeously appareled and live in luxury are in kings' courts. 26 What then did you go out to see? A prophet? Yes, I tell you, and more than a prophet. 27 This is he of whom it is written,
'Behold, I send my messenger before thy face, who shall prepare thy way before thee.'
28 I tell you, among those born of women none is greater than John; yet he who is least in the kingdom of God is greater than he." 29 (When they heard this all the people and the tax collectors justified God, having been baptized with the baptism of John; 30 but the Pharisees and the lawyers rejected the purpose of God for themselves, not having been baptized by him.)
31 "To what then shall I compare the men of this generation, and what are they like? 32 They are like children sitting in the market place and calling to one another,
'We piped to you, and you did not dance; we wailed, and you did not weep.'
33 For John the Baptist has come eating no bread and drinking no wine; and you say, 'He has a demon.' 34 The Son of man has come eating and drinking; and you say, 'Behold, a glutton and a drunkard, a friend

of tax collectors and sinners!' 35 Yet wisdom is justified by all her children."

22.
=====

In Luke 12, Jesus gives "A Warning against Hypocrisy."

12 In the meantime, when so many thousands of the multitude had gathered together that they trod upon one another, he began to say to his disciples first, "Beware of the leaven of the Pharisees, which is hypocrisy. 2 Nothing is covered up that will not be revealed, or hidden that will not be known. 3 Therefore whatever you have said in the dark shall be heard in the light, and what you have whispered in private rooms shall be proclaimed upon the housetops.

23.
=====

In Luke 14, Jesus teaches about "Humility and Hospitality."

7 Now he told a parable to those who were invited, when he marked how they chose the places of honor, saying to them, 8 "When you are invited by any one to a marriage feast, do not sit down in a place of

honor, lest a more eminent man than you be invited by him; 9 and he who invited you both will come and say to you, 'Give place to this man,' and then you will begin with shame to take the lowest place. 10 But when you are invited, go and sit in the lowest place, so that when your host comes he may say to you, 'Friend, go up higher'; then you will be honored in the presence of all who sit at table with you. 11 For every one who exalts himself will be humbled, and he who humbles himself will be exalted."

12 He said also to the man who had invited him, "When you give a dinner or a banquet, do not invite your friends or your brothers or your kinsmen or rich neighbors, lest they also invite you in return, and you be repaid. 13 But when you give a feast, invite the poor, the maimed, the lame, the blind, 14 and you will be blessed, because they cannot repay you. You will be repaid at the resurrection of the just."

24.
=====

In Luke 24, we learn about Jesus and "The Walk to Emmaus."

13 That very day two of them were going to a village named Emma'us, about seven miles[d] from Jerusalem, 14 and talking with each other about all these things that had happened. 15 While they were talking and discussing together, Jesus himself drew

near and went with them. 16 But their eyes were kept from recognizing him. 17 And he said to them, "What is this conversation which you are holding with each other as you walk?" And they stood still, looking sad. 18 Then one of them, named Cle′opas, answered him, "Are you the only visitor to Jerusalem who does not know the things that have happened there in these days?" 19 And he said to them, "What things?" And they said to him, "Concerning Jesus of Nazareth, who was a prophet mighty in deed and word before God and all the people, 20 and how our chief priests and rulers delivered him up to be condemned to death, and crucified him. 21 But we had hoped that he was the one to redeem Israel. Yes, and besides all this, it is now the third day since this happened. 22 Moreover, some women of our company amazed us. They were at the tomb early in the morning 23 and did not find his body; and they came back saying that they had even seen a vision of angels, who said that he was alive. 24 Some of those who were with us went to the tomb, and found it just as the women had said; but him they did not see." 25 And he said to them, "O foolish men, and slow of heart to believe all that the prophets have spoken! 26 Was it not necessary that the Christ should suffer these things and enter into his glory?" 27 And beginning with Moses and all the prophets, he interpreted to them in all the scriptures the things concerning himself.

28 So they drew near to the village to which they were going. He appeared to be going further, 29 but

they constrained him, saying, "Stay with us, for it is toward evening and the day is now far spent." So he went in to stay with them. 30 When he was at table with them, he took the bread and blessed, and broke it, and gave it to them. 31 And their eyes were opened and they recognized him; and he vanished out of their sight. 32 They said to each other, "Did not our hearts burn within us[e] while he talked to us on the road, while he opened to us the scriptures?" 33 And they rose that same hour and returned to Jerusalem; and they found the eleven gathered together and those who were with them, 34 who said, "The Lord has risen indeed, and has appeared to Simon!" 35 Then they told what had happened on the road, and how he was known to them in the breaking of the bread.

25.
=====

In John 3, Jesus teaches about "The One Who Comes from Heaven."

31 He who comes from above is above all; he who is of the earth belongs to the earth, and of the earth he speaks; he who comes from heaven is above all. 32 He bears witness to what he has seen and heard, yet no one receives his testimony; 33 he who receives his testimony sets his seal to this, that God is true. 34 For he whom God has sent utters the words of God, for it is not by measure that he gives the Spirit; 35 the

Father loves the Son, and has given all things into his hand. 36 He who believes in the Son has eternal life; he who does not obey the Son shall not see life, but the wrath of God rests upon him.

26.
=====

In John 4, we learn about "Jesus and the Woman of Samaria."

4 Now when the Lord knew that the Pharisees had heard that Jesus was making and baptizing more disciples than John 2 (although Jesus himself did not baptize, but only his disciples), 3 he left Judea and departed again to Galilee. 4 He had to pass through Samar′ia. 5 So he came to a city of Samar′ia, called Sy′char, near the field that Jacob gave to his son Joseph. 6 Jacob's well was there, and so Jesus, wearied as he was with his journey, sat down beside the well. It was about the sixth hour.
7 There came a woman of Samar′ia to draw water. Jesus said to her, "Give me a drink." 8 For his disciples had gone away into the city to buy food. 9 The Samaritan woman said to him, "How is it that you, a Jew, ask a drink of me, a woman of Samar′ia?" For Jews have no dealings with Samaritans. 10 Jesus answered her, "If you knew the gift of God, and who it is that is saying to you, 'Give me a drink,' you would have asked him, and he would have given you

living water." 11 The woman said to him, "Sir, you have nothing to draw with, and the well is deep; where do you get that living water? 12 Are you greater than our father Jacob, who gave us the well, and drank from it himself, and his sons, and his cattle?" 13 Jesus said to her, "Every one who drinks of this water will thirst again, 14 but whoever drinks of the water that I shall give him will never thirst; the water that I shall give him will become in him a spring of water welling up to eternal life." 15 The woman said to him, "Sir, give me this water, that I may not thirst, nor come here to draw."

16 Jesus said to her, "Go, call your husband, and come here." 17 The woman answered him, "I have no husband." Jesus said to her, "You are right in saying, 'I have no husband'; 18 for you have had five husbands, and he whom you now have is not your husband; this you said truly." 19 The woman said to him, "Sir, I perceive that you are a prophet. 20 Our fathers worshiped on this mountain; and you say that in Jerusalem is the place where men ought to worship." 21 Jesus said to her, "Woman, believe me, the hour is coming when neither on this mountain nor in Jerusalem will you worship the Father. 22 You worship what you do not know; we worship what we know, for salvation is from the Jews. 23 But the hour is coming, and now is, when the true worshipers will worship the Father in spirit and truth, for such the Father seeks to worship him. 24 God is spirit, and those who worship him must worship in spirit and

truth." 25 The woman said to him, "I know that Messiah is coming (he who is called Christ); when he comes, he will show us all things." 26 Jesus said to her, "I who speak to you am he."

27 Just then his disciples came. They marveled that he was talking with a woman, but none said, "What do you wish?" or, "Why are you talking with her?" 28 So the woman left her water jar, and went away into the city, and said to the people, 29 "Come, see a man who told me all that I ever did. Can this be the Christ?" 30 They went out of the city and were coming to him.

31 Meanwhile the disciples besought him, saying, "Rabbi, eat." 32 But he said to them, "I have food to eat of which you do not know." 33 So the disciples said to one another, "Has any one brought him food?" 34 Jesus said to them, "My food is to do the will of him who sent me, and to accomplish his work. 35 Do you not say, 'There are yet four months, then comes the harvest'? I tell you, lift up your eyes, and see how the fields are already white for harvest. 36 He who reaps receives wages, and gathers fruit for eternal life, so that sower and reaper may rejoice together. 37 For here the saying holds true, 'One sows and another reaps.' 38 I sent you to reap that for which you did not labor; others have labored, and you have entered into their labor."

39 Many Samaritans from that city believed in him because of the woman's testimony, "He told me all that I ever did." 40 So when the Samaritans came to

him, they asked him to stay with them; and he stayed there two days. 41 And many more believed because of his word. 42 They said to the woman, "It is no longer because of your words that we believe, for we have heard for ourselves, and we know that this is indeed the Savior of the world."

27.
=====
In John 4, we learn "Jesus Returns to Galilee."

43 After the two days he departed to Galilee. 44 For Jesus himself testified that a prophet has no honor in his own country. 45 So when he came to Galilee, the Galileans welcomed him, having seen all that he had done in Jerusalem at the feast, for they too had gone to the feast.

28.
=====
In John 7, the question arises "Is This the Christ?"

25 Some of the people of Jerusalem therefore said, "Is not this the man whom they seek to kill? 26 And here he is, speaking openly, and they say nothing to him! Can it be that the authorities really know that this is the Christ? 27 Yet we know where this man comes from; and when the Christ appears, no one will know

where he comes from." 28 So Jesus proclaimed, as he taught in the temple, "You know me, and you know where I come from? But I have not come of my own accord; he who sent me is true, and him you do not know. 29 I know him, for I come from him, and he sent me." 30 So they sought to arrest him; but no one laid hands on him, because his hour had not yet come. 31 Yet many of the people believed in him; they said, "When the Christ appears, will he do more signs than this man has done?"

29.
=====

In John 8, we learn about "Jesus the Light of the World."

12 Again Jesus spoke to them, saying, "I am the light of the world; he who follows me will not walk in darkness, but will have the light of life." 13 The Pharisees then said to him, "You are bearing witness to yourself; your testimony is not true." 14 Jesus answered, "Even if I do bear witness to myself, my testimony is true, for I know whence I have come and whither I am going, but you do not know whence I come or whither I am going. 15 You judge according to the flesh, I judge no one. 16 Yet even if I do judge, my judgment is true, for it is not I alone that judge, but I and he[b] who sent me. 17 In your law it is written that the testimony of two men is true; 18 I

bear witness to myself, and the Father who sent me bears witness to me." 19 They said to him therefore, "Where is your Father?" Jesus answered, "You know neither me nor my Father; if you knew me, you would know my Father also." 20 These words he spoke in the treasury, as he taught in the temple; but no one arrested him, because his hour had not yet come.

30.
=====

In John 11, we learn about "The Plot to Kill Jesus."

45 Many of the Jews therefore, who had come with Mary and had seen what he did, believed in him; 46 but some of them went to the Pharisees and told them what Jesus had done. 47 So the chief priests and the Pharisees gathered the council, and said, "What are we to do? For this man performs many signs. 48 If we let him go on thus, every one will believe in him, and the Romans will come and destroy both our holy place[d] and our nation." 49 But one of them, Ca'iaphas, who was high priest that year, said to them, "You know nothing at all; 50 you do not understand that it is expedient for you that one man should die for the people, and that the whole nation should not perish." 51 He did not say this of his own accord, but being high priest that year he prophesied that Jesus should die for the nation, 52 and not for the nation only, but to gather into one the children of God

who are scattered abroad. 53 So from that day on they took counsel how to put him to death.

54 Jesus therefore no longer went about openly among the Jews, but went from there to the country near the wilderness, to a town called E'phraim; and there he stayed with the disciples.

55 Now the Passover of the Jews was at hand, and many went up from the country to Jerusalem before the Passover, to purify themselves. 56 They were looking for Jesus and saying to one another as they stood in the temple, "What do you think? That he will not come to the feast?" 57 Now the chief priests and the Pharisees had given orders that if any one knew where he was, he should let them know, so that they might arrest him.

31.
=====

In John 12, we learn "Some Greeks Wish to See Jesus."

20 Now among those who went up to worship at the feast were some Greeks. 21 So these came to Philip, who was from Beth-sa'ida in Galilee, and said to him, "Sir, we wish to see Jesus." 22 Philip went and told Andrew; Andrew went with Philip and they told Jesus. 23 And Jesus answered them, "The hour has come for the Son of man to be glorified. 24 Truly, truly, I say to you, unless a grain of wheat falls into

the earth and dies, it remains alone; but if it dies, it bears much fruit. 25 He who loves his life loses it, and he who hates his life in this world will keep it for eternal life. 26 If any one serves me, he must follow me; and where I am, there shall my servant be also; if any one serves me, the Father will honor him.

32.
=====

In John 12, we learn about "The Unbelief of the People."

When Jesus had said this, he departed and hid himself from them. 37 Though he had done so many signs before them, yet they did not believe in him; 38 it was that the word spoken by the prophet Isaiah might be fulfilled:
"Lord, who has believed our report,
and to whom has the arm of the Lord been revealed?"
39 Therefore they could not believe. For Isaiah again said,
40 "He has blinded their eyes and hardened their heart,
lest they should see with their eyes and perceive with their heart,
and turn for me to heal them."
41 Isaiah said this because he saw his glory and spoke of him. 42 Nevertheless many even of the authorities believed in him, but for fear of the Pharisees they did

not confess it, lest they should be put out of the synagogue: 43 for they loved the praise of men more than the praise of God.

33.
=====

In John 12, we learn a "Summary of Jesus' Teaching."

44 And Jesus cried out and said, "He who believes in me, believes not in me but in him who sent me. 45 And he who sees me sees him who sent me. 46 I have come as light into the world, that whoever believes in me may not remain in darkness. 47 If any one hears my sayings and does not keep them, I do not judge him; for I did not come to judge the world but to save the world. 48 He who rejects me and does not receive my sayings has a judge; the word that I have spoken will be his judge on the last day. 49 For I have not spoken on my own authority; the Father who sent me has himself given me commandment what to say and what to speak. 50 And I know that his commandment is eternal life. What I say, therefore, I say as the Father has bidden me."

34.
=====

In John 15, Jesus teaches about "The World's Hatred."

18 "If the world hates you, know that it has hated me before it hated you. 19 If you were of the world, the world would love its own; but because you are not of the world, but I chose you out of the world, therefore the world hates you. 20 Remember the word that I said to you, 'A servant[c] is not greater than his master.' If they persecuted me, they will persecute you; if they kept my word, they will keep yours also. 21 But all this they will do to you on my account, because they do not know him who sent me. 22 If I had not come and spoken to them, they would not have sin; but now they have no excuse for their sin. 23 He who hates me hates my Father also. 24 If I had not done among them the works which no one else did, they would not have sin; but now they have seen and hated both me and my Father. 25 It is to fulfil the word that is written in their law, 'They hated me without a cause.' 26 But when the Counselor comes, whom I shall send to you from the Father, even the Spirit of truth, who proceeds from the Father, he will bear witness to me; 27 and you also are witnesses, because you have been with me from the beginning.

35.
=====

In John 17, "Jesus Prays for His Disciples."

17 When Jesus had spoken these words, he lifted up his eyes to heaven and said, "Father, the hour has come; glorify thy Son that the Son may glorify thee, 2 since thou hast given him power over all flesh, to give eternal life to all whom thou hast given him. 3 And this is eternal life, that they know thee the only true God, and Jesus Christ whom thou hast sent. 4 I glorified thee on earth, having accomplished the work which thou gavest me to do; 5 and now, Father, glorify thou me in thy own presence with the glory which I had with thee before the world was made. 6 "I have manifested thy name to the men whom thou gavest me out of the world; thine they were, and thou gavest them to me, and they have kept thy word. 7 Now they know that everything that thou hast given me is from thee; 8 for I have given them the words which thou gavest me, and they have received them and know in truth that I came from thee; and they have believed that thou didst send me. 9 I am praying for them; I am not praying for the world but for those whom thou hast given me, for they are thine; 10 all mine are thine, and thine are mine, and I am glorified in them. 11 And now I am no more in the world, but they are in the world, and I am coming to thee. Holy Father, keep them in thy name, which thou hast given me, that they may be one, even as we are one. 12 While I was with them, I kept them in thy name, which thou hast given me; I have guarded them, and none of them is lost but the son of perdition, that the

scripture might be fulfilled. 13 But now I am coming to thee; and these things I speak in the world, that they may have my joy fulfilled in themselves. 14 I have given them thy word; and the world has hated them because they are not of the world, even as I am not of the world. 15 I do not pray that thou shouldst take them out of the world, but that thou shouldst keep them from the evil one.[a] 16 They are not of the world, even as I am not of the world. 17 Sanctify them in the truth; thy word is truth. 18 As thou didst send me into the world, so I have sent them into the world. 19 And for their sake I consecrate myself, that they also may be consecrated in truth.

20 "I do not pray for these only, but also for those who believe in me through their word, 21 that they may all be one; even as thou, Father, art in me, and I in thee, that they also may be in us, so that the world may believe that thou hast sent me. 22 The glory which thou hast given me I have given to them, that they may be one even as we are one, 23 I in them and thou in me, that they may become perfectly one, so that the world may know that thou hast sent me and hast loved them even as thou hast loved me. 24 Father, I desire that they also, whom thou hast given me, may be with me where I am, to behold my glory which thou hast given me in thy love for me before the foundation of the world. 25 O righteous Father, the world has not known thee, but I have known thee; and these know that thou hast sent me. 26 I made known to them thy name, and I will make it known,

that the love with which thou hast loved me may be in them, and I in them."

36.
=====

In John 18, "The High Priest Questions Jesus."

19 The high priest then questioned Jesus about his disciples and his teaching. 20 Jesus answered him, "I have spoken openly to the world; I have always taught in synagogues and in the temple, where all Jews come together; I have said nothing secretly. 21 Why do you ask me? Ask those who have heard me, what I said to them; they know what I said." 22 When he had said this, one of the officers standing by struck Jesus with his hand, saying, "Is that how you answer the high priest?" 23 Jesus answered him, "If I have spoken wrongly, bear witness to the wrong; but if I have spoken rightly, why do you strike me?" 24 Annas then sent him bound to Ca'iaphas the high priest.

(ii) Supporting Lessons on Fame: 9 Passages

1.

In Matthew 2, we learn about "The Visit of the Wise Men."

2 Now when Jesus was born in Bethlehem of Judea in the days of Herod the king, behold, wise men from the East came to Jerusalem, saying, 2 "Where is he who has been born king of the Jews? For we have seen his star in the East, and have come to worship him." 3 When Herod the king heard this, he was troubled, and all Jerusalem with him; 4 and assembling all the chief priests and scribes of the people, he inquired of them where the Christ was to be born. 5 They told him, "In Bethlehem of Judea; for so it is written by the prophet:
6 'And you, O Bethlehem, in the land of Judah,
are by no means least among the rulers of Judah;
for from you shall come a ruler
who will govern my people Israel.'"
7 Then Herod summoned the wise men secretly and ascertained from them what time the star appeared; 8 and he sent them to Bethlehem, saying, "Go and search diligently for the child, and when you have found him bring me word, that I too may come and worship him." 9 When they had heard the king they went their way; and lo, the star which they had seen in the East went before them, till it came to rest over the place where the child was. 10 When they saw the star, they rejoiced exceedingly with great joy; 11 and going into the house they saw the child with Mary his

mother, and they fell down and worshiped him. Then, opening their treasures, they offered him gifts, gold and frankincense and myrrh. 12 And being warned in a dream not to return to Herod, they departed to their own country by another way.

2.
=====

In Matthew 4 (Mark 1, Luke 4), we learn about "The Temptation of Jesus."

4 Then Jesus was led up by the Spirit into the wilderness to be tempted by the devil. 2 And he fasted forty days and forty nights, and afterward he was hungry. 3 And the tempter came and said to him, "If you are the Son of God, command these stones to become loaves of bread." 4 But he answered, "It is written,
'Man shall not live by bread alone,
but by every word that proceeds from the mouth of God.'"
5 Then the devil took him to the holy city, and set him on the pinnacle of the temple, 6 and said to him, "If you are the Son of God, throw yourself down; for it is written,
'He will give his angels charge of you,'
and
'On their hands they will bear you up,
lest you strike your foot against a stone.'"

Becoming God-like | JTA

7 Jesus said to him, "Again it is written, 'You shall not tempt the Lord your God.'" 8 Again, the devil took him to a very high mountain, and showed him all the kingdoms of the world and the glory of them; 9 and he said to him, "All these I will give you, if you will fall down and worship me." 10 Then Jesus said to him, "Begone, Satan! for it is written,
'You shall worship the Lord your God
and him only shall you serve.'"
11 Then the devil left him, and behold, angels came and ministered to him.

3.
=====

In Matthew 9, "Jesus Heals Two Blind Men."

27 And as Jesus passed on from there, two blind men followed him, crying aloud, "Have mercy on us, Son of David." 28 When he entered the house, the blind men came to him; and Jesus said to them, "Do you believe that I am able to do this?" They said to him, "Yes, Lord." 29 Then he touched their eyes, saying, "According to your faith be it done to you." 30 And their eyes were opened. And Jesus sternly charged them, "See that no one knows it." 31 But they went away and spread his fame through all that district.

4.

=====

In Matthew 21 (Mark 11, Luke 19, John 12), "Jesus' Triumphal Entry into Jerusalem."

21 And when they drew near to Jerusalem and came to Beth′phage, to the Mount of Olives, then Jesus sent two disciples, 2 saying to them, "Go into the village opposite you, and immediately you will find an ass tied, and a colt with her; untie them and bring them to me. 3 If any one says anything to you, you shall say, 'The Lord has need of them,' and he will send them immediately." 4 This took place to fulfil what was spoken by the prophet, saying,
5 "Tell the daughter of Zion,
Behold, your king is coming to you,
humble, and mounted on an ass,
and on a colt, the foal of an ass."
6 The disciples went and did as Jesus had directed them; 7 they brought the ass and the colt, and put their garments on them, and he sat thereon. 8 Most of the crowd spread their garments on the road, and others cut branches from the trees and spread them on the road. 9 And the crowds that went before him and that followed him shouted, "Hosanna to the Son of David! Blessed is he who comes in the name of the Lord! Hosanna in the highest!" 10 And when he entered Jerusalem, all the city was stirred, saying, "Who is this?" 11 And the crowds said, "This is the prophet Jesus from Nazareth of Galilee."

5.
=====

In Mark 3, Jesus is with "A Multitude at the Seaside."

7 Jesus withdrew with his disciples to the sea, and a great multitude from Galilee followed; also from Judea 8 and Jerusalem and Idume'a and from beyond the Jordan and from about Tyre and Sidon a great multitude, hearing all that he did, came to him. 9 And he told his disciples to have a boat ready for him because of the crowd, lest they should crush him; 10 for he had healed many, so that all who had diseases pressed upon him to touch him. 11 And whenever the unclean spirits beheld him, they fell down before him and cried out, "You are the Son of God." 12 And he strictly ordered them not to make him known.

6.
=====

In Mark 7, "Jesus Cures a Deaf Man."

31 Then he returned from the region of Tyre, and went through Sidon to the Sea of Galilee, through the region of the Decap'olis. 32 And they brought to him a man who was deaf and had an impediment in his speech; and they besought him to lay his hand upon him. 33 And taking him aside from the multitude privately, he put his fingers into his ears, and he spat

and touched his tongue; 34 and looking up to heaven, he sighed, and said to him, "Eph'phatha," that is, "Be opened." 35 And his ears were opened, his tongue was released, and he spoke plainly. 36 And he charged them to tell no one; but the more he charged them, the more zealously they proclaimed it. 37 And they were astonished beyond measure, saying, "He has done all things well; he even makes the deaf hear and the dumb speak."

7.
=====

In Luke 9, we learn about "Herod's Perplexity."

7 Now Herod the tetrarch heard of all that was done, and he was perplexed, because it was said by some that John had been raised from the dead, 8 by some that Eli'jah had appeared, and by others that one of the old prophets had risen. 9 Herod said, "John I beheaded; but who is this about whom I hear such things?" And he sought to see him.

8.
=====

In John 2, we learn about Jesus and "The Wedding at Cana."

2 On the third day there was a marriage at Cana in Galilee, and the mother of Jesus was there; 2 Jesus also was invited to the marriage, with his disciples. 3 When the wine gave out, the mother of Jesus said to him, "They have no wine." 4 And Jesus said to her, "O woman, what have you to do with me? My hour has not yet come." 5 His mother said to the servants, "Do whatever he tells you." 6 Now six stone jars were standing there, for the Jewish rites of purification, each holding twenty or thirty gallons. 7 Jesus said to them, "Fill the jars with water." And they filled them up to the brim. 8 He said to them, "Now draw some out, and take it to the steward of the feast." So they took it. 9 When the steward of the feast tasted the water now become wine, and did not know where it came from (though the servants who had drawn the water knew), the steward of the feast called the bridegroom 10 and said to him, "Every man serves the good wine first; and when men have drunk freely, then the poor wine; but you have kept the good wine until now." 11 This, the first of his signs, Jesus did at Cana in Galilee, and manifested his glory; and his disciples believed in him.

12 After this he went down to Caper'na-um, with his mother and his brothers and his disciples; and there they stayed for a few days.

9.

=====

In John 7, we learn about "Division among the People."

40 When they heard these words, some of the people said, "This is really the prophet." 41 Others said, "This is the Christ." But some said, "Is the Christ to come from Galilee? 42 Has not the scripture said that the Christ is descended from David, and comes from Bethlehem, the village where David was?" 43 So there was a division among the people over him. 44 Some of them wanted to arrest him, but no one laid hands on him.

(b) <u>Lessons on Fame from the Acts of the Apostles: List</u>

1. In Acts 2, we learn about "The First Converts."
2. In Acts 5, we learn that "The Apostles Heal Many."
3. In Acts 5, we learn "The Apostles Are Persecuted."
4. In Acts 6, we learn about "Seven Chosen to Serve."

(c) **Lessons on Fame from the Letters: List**

These letters are mostly by Saint Paul, who is known as the Apostle to the Gentiles.

1. In 2 Corinthians 10, we learn that "Paul Defends His Ministry."
2. In 2 Corinthians 11, we learn about "Paul and the False Apostles."
3. In 2 Corinthians 11, we learn about "Paul's Sufferings as an Apostle."
4. In 2 Corinthians 12, we learn about "Paul's Visions and Revelations."
5. In Philippians 2, Paul teaches about "Shining as Lights in the World."
6. In Hebrews 13, we learn about "Service Well-Pleasing to God."
7. In James 3, we learn about "Two Kinds of Wisdom."
8. In James 4, we learn about "Friendship with the World."
9. In James 4, we learn about "Boasting about Tomorrow."

(d) Lessons on Fame from the Revelation to John: List

1. In Revelation 11, we learn about "The Seventh Trumpet."

========================

(6)

GREATNESS

========================

This chapter contains a comprehensive collection of lessons on greatness from Jesus in the Gospels.

The path of greatness is a popular path to happiness, and Jesus and the New Testament have a unique view of greatness. When I worked through the New Testament, I associated ideas like honor and excellence with greatness. In the Synoptic Gospels (Matthew, Mark, Luke), Jesus references the path of greatness often. In the Gospel According to John - the most sublime of the four Gospels - Jesus reflects on greatness, as well, but devotes more time on the blessing of eternal life. The following passages from Jesus in the Gospels are about the path of greatness, which is a popular path to happiness that human beings take in this world.

In the New Testament, after the four Gospels, are the Acts of the Apostles, the Letters, and the Revelation to John. All have much to teach about greatness. However, in this document, I will not cite these remaining passages because the Gospels provide so much already. Also, the remaining material in the New Testament is so rich with material on greatness that to cite them all would make this document quite long. The reader would be better off reading the rest of the New Testament directly for oneself because there is so much in it about greatness.

(a) <u>Lessons on Greatness from Jesus in the Gospels: 40 Passages</u>

(i) Primary Lessons on Greatness: 29 Passages

1-A.
=====

In Matthew 4, we learn how "Jesus Begins His Ministry in Galilee."

12 Now when he heard that John had been arrested, he withdrew into Galilee; 13 and leaving Nazareth he

went and dwelt in Caper'na-um by the sea, in the territory of Zeb'ulun and Naph'tali, 14 that what was spoken by the prophet Isaiah might be fulfilled:
15 "The land of Zeb'ulun and the land of Naph'tali, toward the sea, across the Jordan,
Galilee of the Gentiles—
16 the people who sat in darkness
have seen a great light,
and for those who sat in the region and shadow of death
light has dawned."
17 From that time Jesus began to preach, saying, "Repent, for the kingdom of heaven is at hand."

1-B.
=====

In Mark 1, we learn about Jesus and "The Beginning of the Galilean Ministry."

14 Now after John was arrested, Jesus came into Galilee, preaching the gospel of God, 15 and saying, "The time is fulfilled, and the kingdom of God is at hand; repent, and believe in the gospel."

1-C.
=====

In Luke 4, we learn about Jesus and "The Beginning of the Galilean Ministry."

14 And Jesus returned in the power of the Spirit into Galilee, and a report concerning him went out through all the surrounding country. 15 And he taught in their synagogues, being glorified by all.

2.
=====

In Matthew 5 (Luke 6), Jesus teaches about "The Beatitudes."

5 Seeing the crowds, he went up on the mountain, and when he sat down his disciples came to him. 2 And he opened his mouth and taught them, saying:
3 "Blessed are the poor in spirit, for theirs is the kingdom of heaven.
4 "Blessed are those who mourn, for they shall be comforted.
5 "Blessed are the meek, for they shall inherit the earth.
6 "Blessed are those who hunger and thirst for righteousness, for they shall be satisfied.
7 "Blessed are the merciful, for they shall obtain mercy.
8 "Blessed are the pure in heart, for they shall see God.
9 "Blessed are the peacemakers, for they shall be called sons of God.

10 "Blessed are those who are persecuted for righteousness' sake, for theirs is the kingdom of heaven.
11 "Blessed are you when men revile you and persecute you and utter all kinds of evil against you falsely on my account. 12 Rejoice and be glad, for your reward is great in heaven, for so men persecuted the prophets who were before you.

3.
=====

In Matthew 5, Jesus teaches about "The Law and the Prophets."

17 "Think not that I have come to abolish the law and the prophets; I have come not to abolish them but to fulfil them. 18 For truly, I say to you, till heaven and earth pass away, not an iota, not a dot, will pass from the law until all is accomplished. 19 Whoever then relaxes one of the least of these commandments and teaches men so, shall be called least in the kingdom of heaven; but he who does them and teaches them shall be called great in the kingdom of heaven. 20 For I tell you, unless your righteousness exceeds that of the scribes and Pharisees, you will never enter the kingdom of heaven.

4.

=====

In Matthew 10, Jesus teaches about "Rewards."

40 "He who receives you receives me, and he who receives me receives him who sent me. 41 He who receives a prophet because he is a prophet shall receive a prophet's reward, and he who receives a righteous man because he is a righteous man shall receive a righteous man's reward. 42 And whoever gives to one of these little ones even a cup of cold water because he is a disciple, truly, I say to you, he shall not lose his reward."

5-A.
=====

In Matthew 11, "Jesus Praises John the Baptist."

7 As they went away, Jesus began to speak to the crowds concerning John: "What did you go out into the wilderness to behold? A reed shaken by the wind? 8 Why then did you go out? To see a man[a] clothed in soft raiment? Behold, those who wear soft raiment are in kings' houses. 9 Why then did you go out? To see a prophet?[b] Yes, I tell you, and more than a prophet. 10 This is he of whom it is written,
'Behold, I send my messenger before thy face,
who shall prepare thy way before thee.'
11 Truly, I say to you, among those born of women there has risen no one greater than John the Baptist;

yet he who is least in the kingdom of heaven is greater than he. 12 From the days of John the Baptist until now the kingdom of heaven has suffered violence,[c] and men of violence take it by force. 13 For all the prophets and the law prophesied until John; 14 and if you are willing to accept it, he is Eli'jah who is to come. 15 He who has ears to hear,[d] let him hear.

16 "But to what shall I compare this generation? It is like children sitting in the market places and calling to their playmates,

17 'We piped to you, and you did not dance; we wailed, and you did not mourn.'

18 For John came neither eating nor drinking, and they say, 'He has a demon'; 19 the Son of man came eating and drinking, and they say, 'Behold, a glutton and a drunkard, a friend of tax collectors and sinners!' Yet wisdom is justified by her deeds."[e]

5-B.
=====

In Luke 7, Jesus speaks with "Messengers from John the Baptist."

18 The disciples of John told him of all these things. 19 And John, calling to him two of his disciples, sent them to the Lord, saying, "Are you he who is to come, or shall we look for another?" 20 And when the men had come to him, they said, "John the Baptist

has sent us to you, saying, 'Are you he who is to come, or shall we look for another?'" 21 In that hour he cured many of diseases and plagues and evil spirits, and on many that were blind he bestowed sight. 22 And he answered them, "Go and tell John what you have seen and heard: the blind receive their sight, the lame walk, lepers are cleansed, and the deaf hear, the dead are raised up, the poor have good news preached to them. 23 And blessed is he who takes no offense at me."

24 When the messengers of John had gone, he began to speak to the crowds concerning John: "What did you go out into the wilderness to behold? A reed shaken by the wind? 25 What then did you go out to see? A man clothed in soft clothing? Behold, those who are gorgeously appareled and live in luxury are in kings' courts. 26 What then did you go out to see? A prophet? Yes, I tell you, and more than a prophet. 27 This is he of whom it is written,

'Behold, I send my messenger before thy face, who shall prepare thy way before thee.'

28 I tell you, among those born of women none is greater than John; yet he who is least in the kingdom of God is greater than he." 29 (When they heard this all the people and the tax collectors justified God, having been baptized with the baptism of John; 30 but the Pharisees and the lawyers rejected the purpose of God for themselves, not having been baptized by him.)

31 "To what then shall I compare the men of this generation, and what are they like? 32 They are like children sitting in the market place and calling to one another,
'We piped to you, and you did not dance;
we wailed, and you did not weep.'
33 For John the Baptist has come eating no bread and drinking no wine; and you say, 'He has a demon.' 34 The Son of man has come eating and drinking; and you say, 'Behold, a glutton and a drunkard, a friend of tax collectors and sinners!' 35 Yet wisdom is justified by all her children."

6-A.
=====

In Matthew 11, "Jesus Thanks His Father."

25 At that time Jesus declared, "I thank thee, Father, Lord of heaven and earth, that thou hast hidden these things from the wise and understanding and revealed them to babes; 26 yea, Father, for such was thy gracious will.[f] 27 All things have been delivered to me by my Father; and no one knows the Son except the Father, and no one knows the Father except the Son and any one to whom the Son chooses to reveal him. 28 Come to me, all who labor and are heavy laden, and I will give you rest. 29 Take my yoke upon you, and learn from me; for I am gentle and lowly in

heart, and you will find rest for your souls. 30 For my yoke is easy, and my burden is light."

6-B.
=====
In Luke 10, "Jesus Rejoices."

[Passage begins with "I thank thee, Father" Luke 10:21-22; similar to Mathew 11:25-27]

23 Then turning to the disciples he said privately, "Blessed are the eyes which see what you see! 24 For I tell you that many prophets and kings desired to see what you see, and did not see it, and to hear what you hear, and did not hear it."

7.
=====
In Matthew 16 (Mark 8, Luke 9), we learn about "Peter's Declaration about Jesus."

13 Now when Jesus came into the district of Caesare′a Philippi, he asked his disciples, "Who do men say that the Son of man is?" 14 And they said, "Some say John the Baptist, others say Eli′jah, and others Jeremiah or one of the prophets." 15 He said to them, "But who do you say that I am?" 16 Simon Peter replied, "You are the Christ, the Son of the

living God." 17 And Jesus answered him, "Blessed are you, Simon Bar-Jona! For flesh and blood has not revealed this to you, but my Father who is in heaven. 18 And I tell you, you are Peter,[b] and on this rock[c] I will build my church, and the powers of death[d] shall not prevail against it. 19 I will give you the keys of the kingdom of heaven, and whatever you bind on earth shall be bound in heaven, and whatever you loose on earth shall be loosed in heaven." 20 Then he strictly charged the disciples to tell no one that he was the Christ.

8.
=====

In Matthew 16 (Luke 9), Jesus teaches about "The Cross and Self-Denial."

24 Then Jesus told his disciples, "If any man would come after me, let him deny himself and take up his cross and follow me. 25 For whoever would save his life will lose it, and whoever loses his life for my sake will find it. 26 For what will it profit a man, if he gains the whole world and forfeits his life? Or what shall a man give in return for his life? 27 For the Son of man is to come with his angels in the glory of his Father, and then he will repay every man for what he has done. 28 Truly, I say to you, there are some standing here who will not taste death before they see the Son of man coming in his kingdom."

9-A.

=====

In Matthew 18, Jesus teaches about "True Greatness."

18 At that time the disciples came to Jesus, saying, "Who is the greatest in the kingdom of heaven?" 2 And calling to him a child, he put him in the midst of them, 3 and said, "Truly, I say to you, unless you turn and become like children, you will never enter the kingdom of heaven. 4 Whoever humbles himself like this child, he is the greatest in the kingdom of heaven.

9-B.

=====

In Mark 9, Jesus teaches about "Who Is the Greatest?"

33 And they came to Caper'na-um; and when he was in the house he asked them, "What were you discussing on the way?" 34 But they were silent; for on the way they had discussed with one another who was the greatest. 35 And he sat down and called the twelve; and he said to them, "If any one would be first, he must be last of all and servant of all." 36 And he took a child, and put him in the midst of them; and taking him in his arms, he said to them, 37 "Whoever receives one such child in my name receives me; and

whoever receives me, receives not me but him who sent me."

9-C.
=====

In Luke 9, Jesus teaches about "True Greatness."

46 And an argument arose among them as to which of them was the greatest. 47 But when Jesus perceived the thought of their hearts, he took a child and put him by his side, 48 and said to them, "Whoever receives this child in my name receives me, and whoever receives me receives him who sent me; for he who is least among you all is the one who is great."

9-D.
=====

In Luke 22, Jesus answers "The Dispute about Greatness."

24 A dispute also arose among them, which of them was to be regarded as the greatest. 25 And he said to them, "The kings of the Gentiles exercise lordship over them; and those in authority over them are called benefactors. 26 But not so with you; rather let the greatest among you become as the youngest, and the leader as one who serves. 27 For which is the greater,

one who sits at table, or one who serves? Is it not the one who sits at table? But I am among you as one who serves.
28 "You are those who have continued with me in my trials; 29 and I assign to you, as my Father assigned to me, a kingdom, 30 that you may eat and drink at my table in my kingdom, and sit on thrones judging the twelve tribes of Israel.

10.
=====

In Matthew 21 (Mark 11, Luke 19, John 12), we learn about "Jesus' Triumphal Entry into Jerusalem."

21 And when they drew near to Jerusalem and came to Beth′phage, to the Mount of Olives, then Jesus sent two disciples, 2 saying to them, "Go into the village opposite you, and immediately you will find an ass tied, and a colt with her; untie them and bring them to me. 3 If any one says anything to you, you shall say, 'The Lord has need of them,' and he will send them immediately." 4 This took place to fulfil what was spoken by the prophet, saying,
5 "Tell the daughter of Zion,
Behold, your king is coming to you,
humble, and mounted on an ass,
and on a colt, the foal of an ass."
6 The disciples went and did as Jesus had directed them; 7 they brought the ass and the colt, and put

their garments on them, and he sat thereon. 8 Most of the crowd spread their garments on the road, and others cut branches from the trees and spread them on the road. 9 And the crowds that went before him and that followed him shouted, "Hosanna to the Son of David! Blessed is he who comes in the name of the Lord! Hosanna in the highest!" 10 And when he entered Jerusalem, all the city was stirred, saying, "Who is this?" 11 And the crowds said, "This is the prophet Jesus from Nazareth of Galilee."

11.
=====

In Matthew 23 (Mark 12, Luke 11, Luke 20), "Jesus Denounces Scribes and Pharisees."

23 Then said Jesus to the crowds and to his disciples, 2 "The scribes and the Pharisees sit on Moses' seat; 3 so practice and observe whatever they tell you, but not what they do; for they preach, but do not practice. 4 They bind heavy burdens, hard to bear,[a] and lay them on men's shoulders; but they themselves will not move them with their finger. 5 They do all their deeds to be seen by men; for they make their phylacteries broad and their fringes long, 6 and they love the place of honor at feasts and the best seats in the synagogues, 7 and salutations in the market places, and being called rabbi by men. 8 But you are not to be called rabbi, for you have one teacher, and

you are all brethren. 9 And call no man your father on earth, for you have one Father, who is in heaven. 10 Neither be called masters, for you have one master, the Christ. 11 He who is greatest among you shall be your servant; 12 whoever exalts himself will be humbled, and whoever humbles himself will be exalted.

13 "But woe to you, scribes and Pharisees, hypocrites! because you shut the kingdom of heaven against men; for you neither enter yourselves, nor allow those who would enter to go in.[b] 15 Woe to you, scribes and Pharisees, hypocrites! for you traverse sea and land to make a single proselyte, and when he becomes a proselyte, you make him twice as much a child of hell[c] as yourselves.

16 "Woe to you, blind guides, who say, 'If any one swears by the temple, it is nothing; but if any one swears by the gold of the temple, he is bound by his oath.' 17 You blind fools! For which is greater, the gold or the temple that has made the gold sacred? 18 And you say, 'If any one swears by the altar, it is nothing; but if any one swears by the gift that is on the altar, he is bound by his oath.' 19 You blind men! For which is greater, the gift or the altar that makes the gift sacred? 20 So he who swears by the altar, swears by it and by everything on it; 21 and he who swears by the temple, swears by it and by him who dwells in it; 22 and he who swears by heaven, swears by the throne of God and by him who sits upon it.

23 "Woe to you, scribes and Pharisees, hypocrites! for you tithe mint and dill and cummin, and have neglected the weightier matters of the law, justice and mercy and faith; these you ought to have done, without neglecting the others. 24 You blind guides, straining out a gnat and swallowing a camel!
25 "Woe to you, scribes and Pharisees, hypocrites! for you cleanse the outside of the cup and of the plate, but inside they are full of extortion and rapacity. 26 You blind Pharisee! first cleanse the inside of the cup and of the plate, that the outside also may be clean.
27 "Woe to you, scribes and Pharisees, hypocrites! for you are like whitewashed tombs, which outwardly appear beautiful, but within they are full of dead men's bones and all uncleanness. 28 So you also outwardly appear righteous to men, but within you are full of hypocrisy and iniquity.
29 "Woe to you, scribes and Pharisees, hypocrites! for you build the tombs of the prophets and adorn the monuments of the righteous, 30 saying, 'If we had lived in the days of our fathers, we would not have taken part with them in shedding the blood of the prophets.' 31 Thus you witness against yourselves, that you are sons of those who murdered the prophets. 32 Fill up, then, the measure of your fathers. 33 You serpents, you brood of vipers, how are you to escape being sentenced to hell?[d] 34 Therefore I send you prophets and wise men and scribes, some of whom you will kill and crucify, and some you will scourge in your synagogues and persecute from town to town,

35 that upon you may come all the righteous blood shed on earth, from the blood of innocent Abel to the blood of Zechari'ah the son of Barachi'ah, whom you murdered between the sanctuary and the altar. 36 Truly, I say to you, all this will come upon this generation.

12.
=====

In Matthew 24 (Mark 13), Jesus teaches about "The Coming of the Son of Man."

29 "Immediately after the tribulation of those days the sun will be darkened, and the moon will not give its light, and the stars will fall from heaven, and the powers of the heavens will be shaken; 30 then will appear the sign of the Son of man in heaven, and then all the tribes of the earth will mourn, and they will see the Son of man coming on the clouds of heaven with power and great glory; 31 and he will send out his angels with a loud trumpet call, and they will gather his elect from the four winds, from one end of heaven to the other.

13.
=====

In Matthew 25, Jesus teaches about "The Judgment of the Nations."

31 "When the Son of man comes in his glory, and all the angels with him, then he will sit on his glorious throne. 32 Before him will be gathered all the nations, and he will separate them one from another as a shepherd separates the sheep from the goats, 33 and he will place the sheep at his right hand, but the goats at the left. 34 Then the King will say to those at his right hand, 'Come, O blessed of my Father, inherit the kingdom prepared for you from the foundation of the world; 35 for I was hungry and you gave me food, I was thirsty and you gave me drink, I was a stranger and you welcomed me, 36 I was naked and you clothed me, I was sick and you visited me, I was in prison and you came to me.' 37 Then the righteous will answer him, 'Lord, when did we see thee hungry and feed thee, or thirsty and give thee drink? 38 And when did we see thee a stranger and welcome thee, or naked and clothe thee? 39 And when did we see thee sick or in prison and visit thee?' 40 And the King will answer them, 'Truly, I say to you, as you did it to one of the least of these my brethren, you did it to me.' 41 Then he will say to those at his left hand, 'Depart from me, you cursed, into the eternal fire prepared for the devil and his angels; 42 for I was hungry and you gave me no food, I was thirsty and you gave me no drink, 43 I was a stranger and you did not welcome me, naked and you did not clothe me, sick and in prison and you did not visit me.' 44 Then they also will answer, 'Lord, when did we see thee hungry or

thirsty or a stranger or naked or sick or in prison, and did not minister to thee?' 45 Then he will answer them, 'Truly, I say to you, as you did it not to one of the least of these, you did it not to me.' 46 And they will go away into eternal punishment, but the righteous into eternal life."

14.
=====

In Mark 10 (Matthew 19, Luke 18), "Jesus Blesses Little Children."

13 And they were bringing children to him, that he might touch them; and the disciples rebuked them. 14 But when Jesus saw it he was indignant, and said to them, "Let the children come to me, do not hinder them; for to such belongs the kingdom of God. 15 Truly, I say to you, whoever does not receive the kingdom of God like a child shall not enter it." 16 And he took them in his arms and blessed them, laying his hands upon them.

15.
=====

In Mark 10 (Matthew 20), Jesus answers "The Request of James and John."

35 And James and John, the sons of Zeb′edee, came forward to him, and said to him, "Teacher, we want you to do for us whatever we ask of you." 36 And he said to them, "What do you want me to do for you?" 37 And they said to him, "Grant us to sit, one at your right hand and one at your left, in your glory." 38 But Jesus said to them, "You do not know what you are asking. Are you able to drink the cup that I drink, or to be baptized with the baptism with which I am baptized?" 39 And they said to him, "We are able." And Jesus said to them, "The cup that I drink you will drink; and with the baptism with which I am baptized, you will be baptized; 40 but to sit at my right hand or at my left is not mine to grant, but it is for those for whom it has been prepared." 41 And when the ten heard it, they began to be indignant at James and John. 42 And Jesus called them to him and said to them, "You know that those who are supposed to rule over the Gentiles lord it over them, and their great men exercise authority over them. 43 But it shall not be so among you; but whoever would be great among you must be your servant, 44 and whoever would be first among you must be slave of all. 45 For the Son of man also came not to be served but to serve, and to give his life as a ransom for many."

16.
=====

In Mark 12 (Matthew 22), Jesus teaches about "The First Commandment."

28 And one of the scribes came up and heard them disputing with one another, and seeing that he answered them well, asked him, "Which commandment is the first of all?" 29 Jesus answered, "The first is, 'Hear, O Israel: The Lord our God, the Lord is one; 30 and you shall love the Lord your God with all your heart, and with all your soul, and with all your mind, and with all your strength.' 31 The second is this, 'You shall love your neighbor as yourself.' There is no other commandment greater than these." 32 And the scribe said to him, "You are right, Teacher; you have truly said that he is one, and there is no other but he; 33 and to love him with all the heart, and with all the understanding, and with all the strength, and to love one's neighbor as oneself, is much more than all whole burnt offerings and sacrifices." 34 And when Jesus saw that he answered wisely, he said to him, "You are not far from the kingdom of God." And after that no one dared to ask him any question.

17.
=====
In Mark 12 (Matthew 22, Luke 20), Jesus proposes "The Question about David's Son."

35 And as Jesus taught in the temple, he said, "How can the scribes say that the Christ is the son of David? 36 David himself, inspired by[c] the Holy Spirit, declared,
'The Lord said to my Lord,
Sit at my right hand,
till I put thy enemies under thy feet.'
37 David himself calls him Lord; so how is he his son?" And the great throng heard him gladly.

18.
=====

In Luke 3 (Matthew 3, Mark 1), we learn about "The Proclamation of John the Baptist."

3 In the fifteenth year of the reign of Tibe′ri-us Caesar, Pontius Pilate being governor of Judea, and Herod being tetrarch of Galilee, and his brother Philip tetrarch of the region of Iturae′a and Trachoni′tis, and Lysa′ni-as tetrarch of Abile′ne, 2 in the high-priesthood of Annas and Ca′iaphas, the word of God came to John the son of Zechari′ah in the wilderness; 3 and he went into all the region about the Jordan, preaching a baptism of repentance for the forgiveness of sins. 4 As it is written in the book of the words of Isaiah the prophet,
"The voice of one crying in the wilderness:
Prepare the way of the Lord,
make his paths straight.

5 Every valley shall be filled,
and every mountain and hill shall be brought low,
and the crooked shall be made straight,
and the rough ways shall be made smooth;
6 and all flesh shall see the salvation of God."
7 He said therefore to the multitudes that came out to be baptized by him, "You brood of vipers! Who warned you to flee from the wrath to come? 8 Bear fruits that befit repentance, and do not begin to say to yourselves, 'We have Abraham as our father'; for I tell you, God is able from these stones to raise up children to Abraham. 9 Even now the axe is laid to the root of the trees; every tree therefore that does not bear good fruit is cut down and thrown into the fire." 10 And the multitudes asked him, "What then shall we do?" 11 And he answered them, "He who has two coats, let him share with him who has none; and he who has food, let him do likewise." 12 Tax collectors also came to be baptized, and said to him, "Teacher, what shall we do?" 13 And he said to them, "Collect no more than is appointed you." 14 Soldiers also asked him, "And we, what shall we do?" And he said to them, "Rob no one by violence or by false accusation, and be content with your wages."
15 As the people were in expectation, and all men questioned in their hearts concerning John, whether perhaps he were the Christ, 16 John answered them all, "I baptize you with water; but he who is mightier than I is coming, the thong of whose sandals I am not worthy to untie; he will baptize you with the Holy

Spirit and with fire. 17 His winnowing fork is in his hand, to clear his threshing floor, and to gather the wheat into his granary, but the chaff he will burn with unquenchable fire."

18 So, with many other exhortations, he preached good news to the people. 19 But Herod the tetrarch, who had been reproved by him for Hero′di-as, his brother's wife, and for all the evil things that Herod had done, 20 added this to them all, that he shut up John in prison.

19.
=====

In Luke 6 (Matthew 5), Jesus teaches about "Love for Enemies."

27 "But I say to you that hear, Love your enemies, do good to those who hate you, 28 bless those who curse you, pray for those who abuse you. 29 To him who strikes you on the cheek, offer the other also; and from him who takes away your coat do not withhold even your shirt. 30 Give to every one who begs from you; and of him who takes away your goods do not ask them again. 31 And as you wish that men would do to you, do so to them.

32 "If you love those who love you, what credit is that to you? For even sinners love those who love them. 33 And if you do good to those who do good to you, what credit is that to you? For even sinners do

the same. 34 And if you lend to those from whom you hope to receive, what credit is that to you? Even sinners lend to sinners, to receive as much again. 35 But love your enemies, and do good, and lend, expecting nothing in return;[b] and your reward will be great, and you will be sons of the Most High; for he is kind to the ungrateful and the selfish. 36 Be merciful, even as your Father is merciful.

20.
======

In Luke 6, Jesus teaches about "Judging Others."

37 "Judge not, and you will not be judged; condemn not, and you will not be condemned; forgive, and you will be forgiven; 38 give, and it will be given to you; good measure, pressed down, shaken together, running over, will be put into your lap. For the measure you give will be the measure you get back." 39 He also told them a parable: "Can a blind man lead a blind man? Will they not both fall into a pit? 40 A disciple is not above his teacher, but every one when he is fully taught will be like his teacher. 41 Why do you see the speck that is in your brother's eye, but do not notice the log that is in your own eye? 42 Or how can you say to your brother, 'Brother, let me take out the speck that is in your eye,' when you yourself do not see the log that is in your own eye? You hypocrite, first take the log out of your own eye, and

then you will see clearly to take out the speck that is in your brother's eye.

21.
=====

In Luke 10, Jesus teaches "The Parable of the Good Samaritan."

25 And behold, a lawyer stood up to put him to the test, saying, "Teacher, what shall I do to inherit eternal life?" 26 He said to him, "What is written in the law? How do you read?" 27 And he answered, "You shall love the Lord your God with all your heart, and with all your soul, and with all your strength, and with all your mind; and your neighbor as yourself." 28 And he said to him, "You have answered right; do this, and you will live."
29 But he, desiring to justify himself, said to Jesus, "And who is my neighbor?" 30 Jesus replied, "A man was going down from Jerusalem to Jericho, and he fell among robbers, who stripped him and beat him, and departed, leaving him half dead. 31 Now by chance a priest was going down that road; and when he saw him he passed by on the other side. 32 So likewise a Levite, when he came to the place and saw him, passed by on the other side. 33 But a Samaritan, as he journeyed, came to where he was; and when he saw him, he had compassion, 34 and went to him and bound up his wounds, pouring on oil and wine; then

he set him on his own beast and brought him to an inn, and took care of him. 35 And the next day he took out two denarii[d] and gave them to the innkeeper, saying, 'Take care of him; and whatever more you spend, I will repay you when I come back.' 36 Which of these three, do you think, proved neighbor to the man who fell among the robbers?" 37 He said, "The one who showed mercy on him." And Jesus said to him, "Go and do likewise."

22.
=====

In Luke 11, Jesus teaches about "True Blessedness."

27 As he said this, a woman in the crowd raised her voice and said to him, "Blessed is the womb that bore you, and the breasts that you sucked!" 28 But he said, "Blessed rather are those who hear the word of God and keep it!"

23.
=====

In Luke 12, Jesus teaches about "Watchful Slaves."

35 "Let your loins be girded and your lamps burning, 36 and be like men who are waiting for their master to come home from the marriage feast, so that they may open to him at once when he comes and knocks.

37 Blessed are those servants whom the master finds awake when he comes; truly, I say to you, he will gird himself and have them sit at table, and he will come and serve them. 38 If he comes in the second watch, or in the third, and finds them so, blessed are those servants! 39 But know this, that if the householder had known at what hour the thief was coming, he[e] would not have left his house to be broken into. 40 You also must be ready; for the Son of man is coming at an unexpected hour."

24.
=====

In Luke 14, Jesus teaches about "Humility and Hospitality."

7 Now he told a parable to those who were invited, when he marked how they chose the places of honor, saying to them, 8 "When you are invited by any one to a marriage feast, do not sit down in a place of honor, lest a more eminent man than you be invited by him; 9 and he who invited you both will come and say to you, 'Give place to this man,' and then you will begin with shame to take the lowest place. 10 But when you are invited, go and sit in the lowest place, so that when your host comes he may say to you, 'Friend, go up higher'; then you will be honored in the presence of all who sit at table with you. 11 For

every one who exalts himself will be humbled, and he who humbles himself will be exalted."

12 He said also to the man who had invited him, "When you give a dinner or a banquet, do not invite your friends or your brothers or your kinsmen or rich neighbors, lest they also invite you in return, and you be repaid. 13 But when you give a feast, invite the poor, the maimed, the lame, the blind, 14 and you will be blessed, because they cannot repay you. You will be repaid at the resurrection of the just."

25.
=====

In Luke 18, Jesus teaches "The Parable of the Pharisee and the Tax Collector."

9 He also told this parable to some who trusted in themselves that they were righteous and despised others: 10 "Two men went up into the temple to pray, one a Pharisee and the other a tax collector. 11 The Pharisee stood and prayed thus with himself, 'God, I thank thee that I am not like other men, extortioners, unjust, adulterers, or even like this tax collector. 12 I fast twice a week, I give tithes of all that I get.' 13 But the tax collector, standing far off, would not even lift up his eyes to heaven, but beat his breast, saying, 'God, be merciful to me a sinner!' 14 I tell you, this man went down to his house justified rather than the other; for every one who exalts himself will be

humbled, but he who humbles himself will be exalted."

26.
=====

In John 10, "Jesus Is Rejected by the Jews."

22 It was the feast of the Dedication at Jerusalem; 23 it was winter, and Jesus was walking in the temple, in the portico of Solomon. 24 So the Jews gathered round him and said to him, "How long will you keep us in suspense? If you are the Christ, tell us plainly." 25 Jesus answered them, "I told you, and you do not believe. The works that I do in my Father's name, they bear witness to me; 26 but you do not believe, because you do not belong to my sheep. 27 My sheep hear my voice, and I know them, and they follow me; 28 and I give them eternal life, and they shall never perish, and no one shall snatch them out of my hand. 29 My Father, who has given them to me,[a] is greater than all, and no one is able to snatch them out of the Father's hand. 30 I and the Father are one." 31 The Jews took up stones again to stone him. 32 Jesus answered them, "I have shown you many good works from the Father; for which of these do you stone me?" 33 The Jews answered him, "It is not for a good work that we stone you but for blasphemy; because you, being a man, make yourself God." 34 Jesus answered them, "Is it not written in your law, 'I

said, you are gods'? 35 If he called them gods to whom the word of God came (and scripture cannot be broken), 36 do you say of him whom the Father consecrated and sent into the world, 'You are blaspheming,' because I said, 'I am the Son of God'? 37 If I am not doing the works of my Father, then do not believe me; 38 but if I do them, even though you do not believe me, believe the works, that you may know and understand that the Father is in me and I am in the Father." 39 Again they tried to arrest him, but he escaped from their hands.

40 He went away again across the Jordan to the place where John at first baptized, and there he remained. 41 And many came to him; and they said, "John did no sign, but everything that John said about this man was true." 42 And many believed in him there.

27.
=====

In John 12, "Jesus Speaks about His Death."

27 "Now is my soul troubled. And what shall I say? 'Father, save me from this hour'? No, for this purpose I have come to this hour. 28 Father, glorify thy name." Then a voice came from heaven, "I have glorified it, and I will glorify it again." 29 The crowd standing by heard it and said that it had thundered. Others said, "An angel has spoken to him." 30 Jesus answered, "This voice has come for your sake, not for

mine. 31 Now is the judgment of this world, now shall the ruler of this world be cast out; 32 and I, when I am lifted up from the earth, will draw all men to myself." 33 He said this to show by what death he was to die. 34 The crowd answered him, "We have heard from the law that the Christ remains for ever. How can you say that the Son of man must be lifted up? Who is this Son of man?" 35 Jesus said to them, "The light is with you for a little longer. Walk while you have the light, lest the darkness overtake you; he who walks in the darkness does not know where he goes. 36 While you have the light, believe in the light, that you may become sons of light."

28.
=====

In John 13, "Jesus Washes the Disciples' Feet."

13 Now before the feast of the Passover, when Jesus knew that his hour had come to depart out of this world to the Father, having loved his own who were in the world, he loved them to the end. 2 And during supper, when the devil had already put it into the heart of Judas Iscariot, Simon's son, to betray him, 3 Jesus, knowing that the Father had given all things into his hands, and that he had come from God and was going to God, 4 rose from supper, laid aside his garments, and girded himself with a towel. 5 Then he poured water into a basin, and began to wash the

disciples' feet, and to wipe them with the towel with which he was girded. 6 He came to Simon Peter; and Peter said to him, "Lord, do you wash my feet?" 7 Jesus answered him, "What I am doing you do not know now, but afterward you will understand." 8 Peter said to him, "You shall never wash my feet." Jesus answered him, "If I do not wash you, you have no part in me." 9 Simon Peter said to him, "Lord, not my feet only but also my hands and my head!" 10 Jesus said to him, "He who has bathed does not need to wash, except for his feet,[a] but he is clean all over; and you[b] are clean, but not every one of you." 11 For he knew who was to betray him; that was why he said, "You are not all clean."

12 When he had washed their feet, and taken his garments, and resumed his place, he said to them, "Do you know what I have done to you? 13 You call me Teacher and Lord; and you are right, for so I am. 14 If I then, your Lord and Teacher, have washed your feet, you also ought to wash one another's feet. 15 For I have given you an example, that you also should do as I have done to you. 16 Truly, truly, I say to you, a servant[c] is not greater than his master; nor is he who is sent greater than he who sent him. 17 If you know these things, blessed are you if you do them. 18 I am not speaking of you all; I know whom I have chosen; it is that the scripture may be fulfilled, 'He who ate my bread has lifted his heel against me.' 19 I tell you this now, before it takes place, that when it does take place you may believe that I am he. 20

Truly, truly, I say to you, he who receives any one whom I send receives me; and he who receives me receives him who sent me."

29.
=====

In John 13, Jesus teaches "The New Commandment."

31 When he had gone out, Jesus said, "Now is the Son of man glorified, and in him God is glorified; 32 if God is glorified in him, God will also glorify him in himself, and glorify him at once. 33 Little children, yet a little while I am with you. You will seek me; and as I said to the Jews so now I say to you, 'Where I am going you cannot come.' 34 A new commandment I give to you, that you love one another; even as I have loved you, that you also love one another. 35 By this all men will know that you are my disciples, if you have love for one another."

(ii) Supporting Lessons on Greatness: 11 Passages

1.
=====

In Matthew 3 (Mark 1, Luke 3), we learn about "The Baptism of Jesus."

13 Then Jesus came from Galilee to the Jordan to John, to be baptized by him. 14 John would have prevented him, saying, "I need to be baptized by you, and do you come to me?" 15 But Jesus answered him, "Let it be so now; for thus it is fitting for us to fulfil all righteousness." Then he consented. 16 And when Jesus was baptized, he went up immediately from the water, and behold, the heavens were opened[a] and he saw the Spirit of God descending like a dove, and alighting on him; 17 and lo, a voice from heaven, saying, "This is my beloved Son,[b] with whom I am well pleased."

2.
=====

In Matthew 4 (Mark 1, Luke 4), we learn about "The Temptation of Jesus."

4 Then Jesus was led up by the Spirit into the wilderness to be tempted by the devil. 2 And he fasted forty days and forty nights, and afterward he was hungry. 3 And the tempter came and said to him, "If you are the Son of God, command these stones to become loaves of bread." 4 But he answered, "It is written,
'Man shall not live by bread alone,

but by every word that proceeds from the mouth of God.'"

5 Then the devil took him to the holy city, and set him on the pinnacle of the temple, 6 and said to him, "If you are the Son of God, throw yourself down; for it is written,

'He will give his angels charge of you,'
and
'On their hands they will bear you up,
lest you strike your foot against a stone.'"

7 Jesus said to him, "Again it is written, 'You shall not tempt the Lord your God.'" 8 Again, the devil took him to a very high mountain, and showed him all the kingdoms of the world and the glory of them; 9 and he said to him, "All these I will give you, if you will fall down and worship me." 10 Then Jesus said to him, "Begone, Satan! for it is written,

'You shall worship the Lord your God
and him only shall you serve.'"

11 Then the devil left him, and behold, angels came and ministered to him.

3.
=====

In Matthew 4 (Mark 1, Luke 5), "Jesus Calls the First Disciples."

18 As he walked by the Sea of Galilee, he saw two brothers, Simon who is called Peter and Andrew his

brother, casting a net into the sea; for they were fishermen. 19 And he said to them, "Follow me, and I will make you fishers of men." 20 Immediately they left their nets and followed him. 21 And going on from there he saw two other brothers, James the son of Zeb'edee and John his brother, in the boat with Zeb'edee their father, mending their nets, and he called them. 22 Immediately they left the boat and their father, and followed him.

4.
=====

In Matthew 20, Jesus teaches about "The Laborers in the Vineyard."

20 "For the kingdom of heaven is like a householder who went out early in the morning to hire laborers for his vineyard. 2 After agreeing with the laborers for a denarius[a] a day, he sent them into his vineyard. 3 And going out about the third hour he saw others standing idle in the market place; 4 and to them he said, 'You go into the vineyard too, and whatever is right I will give you.' So they went. 5 Going out again about the sixth hour and the ninth hour, he did the same. 6 And about the eleventh hour he went out and found others standing; and he said to them, 'Why do you stand here idle all day?' 7 They said to him, 'Because no one has hired us.' He said to them, 'You go into the vineyard too.' 8 And when evening came,

the owner of the vineyard said to his steward, 'Call the laborers and pay them their wages, beginning with the last, up to the first.' 9 And when those hired about the eleventh hour came, each of them received a denarius. 10 Now when the first came, they thought they would receive more; but each of them also received a denarius. 11 And on receiving it they grumbled at the householder, 12 saying, 'These last worked only one hour, and you have made them equal to us who have borne the burden of the day and the scorching heat.' 13 But he replied to one of them, 'Friend, I am doing you no wrong; did you not agree with me for a denarius? 14 Take what belongs to you, and go; I choose to give to this last as I give to you. 15 Am I not allowed to do what I choose with what belongs to me? Or do you begrudge my generosity?'[b] 16 So the last will be first, and the first last."

5.
=====

In Matthew 25 (Luke 19), Jesus teaches "The Parable of the Talents."

14 "For it will be as when a man going on a journey called his servants and entrusted to them his property; 15 to one he gave five talents,[b] to another two, to another one, to each according to his ability. Then he went away. 16 He who had received the five talents

went at once and traded with them; and he made five talents more. 17 So also, he who had the two talents made two talents more. 18 But he who had received the one talent went and dug in the ground and hid his master's money. 19 Now after a long time the master of those servants came and settled accounts with them. 20 And he who had received the five talents came forward, bringing five talents more, saying, 'Master, you delivered to me five talents; here I have made five talents more.' 21 His master said to him, 'Well done, good and faithful servant; you have been faithful over a little, I will set you over much; enter into the joy of your master.' 22 And he also who had the two talents came forward, saying, 'Master, you delivered to me two talents; here I have made two talents more.' 23 His master said to him, 'Well done, good and faithful servant; you have been faithful over a little, I will set you over much; enter into the joy of your master.' 24 He also who had received the one talent came forward, saying, 'Master, I knew you to be a hard man, reaping where you did not sow, and gathering where you did not winnow; 25 so I was afraid, and I went and hid your talent in the ground. Here you have what is yours.' 26 But his master answered him, 'You wicked and slothful servant! You knew that I reap where I have not sowed, and gather where I have not winnowed? 27 Then you ought to have invested my money with the bankers, and at my coming I should have received what was my own with interest. 28 So take the talent from him, and give it to him who has the ten talents. 29 For to every one who has will more be given, and he will have abundance; but from him who has not, even what he has will be taken away. 30 And cast the worthless servant into the outer darkness; there men will weep and gnash their teeth.'

6.
=====
In Luke 1, we learn about "The Birth of Jesus Foretold."

26 In the sixth month the angel Gabriel was sent from God to a city of Galilee named Nazareth, 27 to a virgin betrothed to a man whose name was Joseph, of the house of David; and the virgin's name was Mary. 28 And he came to her and said, "Hail, O favored one, the Lord is with you!"[c] 29 But she was greatly troubled at the saying, and considered in her mind what sort of greeting this might be. 30 And the angel said to her, "Do not be afraid, Mary, for you have found favor with God. 31 And behold, you will conceive in your womb and bear a son, and you shall call his name Jesus.
32 He will be great, and will be called the Son of the Most High;
and the Lord God will give to him the throne of his father David,
33 and he will reign over the house of Jacob for ever;

and of his kingdom there will be no end."
34 And Mary said to the angel, "How shall this be, since I have no husband?" 35 And the angel said to her,
"The Holy Spirit will come upon you,
and the power of the Most High will overshadow you;
therefore the child to be born[d] will be called holy, the Son of God.
36 And behold, your kinswoman Elizabeth in her old age has also conceived a son; and this is the sixth month with her who was called barren. 37 For with God nothing will be impossible." 38 And Mary said, "Behold, I am the handmaid of the Lord; let it be to me according to your word." And the angel departed from her.

7.
=====

In Luke 1, we learn about "Mary's Song of Praise."

"My soul magnifies the Lord,
47 and my spirit rejoices in God my Savior,
48 for he has regarded the low estate of his handmaiden.
For behold, henceforth all generations will call me blessed;
49 for he who is mighty has done great things for me, and holy is his name.
50 And his mercy is on those who fear him

from generation to generation.
51 He has shown strength with his arm,
he has scattered the proud in the imagination of their hearts,
52 he has put down the mighty from their thrones,
and exalted those of low degree;
53 he has filled the hungry with good things,
and the rich he has sent empty away.
54 He has helped his servant Israel,
in remembrance of his mercy,
55 as he spoke to our fathers,
to Abraham and to his posterity for ever."
56 And Mary remained with her about three months, and returned to her home.

8.
=====

In Luke 1, we learn about "Zechariah's Prophecy."

67 And his [John the Baptist's] father Zechari'ah was filled with the Holy Spirit, and prophesied, saying,
68 "Blessed be the Lord God of Israel,
for he has visited and redeemed his people,
69 and has raised up a horn of salvation for us
in the house of his servant David,
70 as he spoke by the mouth of his holy prophets from of old,
71 that we should be saved from our enemies,
and from the hand of all who hate us;

72 to perform the mercy promised to our fathers,
and to remember his holy covenant,
73 the oath which he swore to our father Abraham, 74 to grant us
that we, being delivered from the hand of our enemies,
might serve him without fear,
75 in holiness and righteousness before him all the days of our life.
76 And you, child, will be called the prophet of the Most High;
for you will go before the Lord to prepare his ways,
77 to give knowledge of salvation to his people
in the forgiveness of their sins,
78 through the tender mercy of our God,
when the day shall dawn upon[f] us from on high
79 to give light to those who sit in darkness and in the shadow of death,
to guide our feet into the way of peace."
80 And the child grew and became strong in spirit,
and he was in the wilderness till the day of his manifestation to Israel.

9.

======

In Luke 2, we learn about Jesus' birth with "The Shepherds and the Angels."

8 And in that region there were shepherds out in the field, keeping watch over their flock by night. 9 And an angel of the Lord appeared to them, and the glory of the Lord shone around them, and they were filled with fear. 10 And the angel said to them, "Be not afraid; for behold, I bring you good news of a great joy which will come to all the people; 11 for to you is born this day in the city of David a Savior, who is Christ the Lord. 12 And this will be a sign for you: you will find a babe wrapped in swaddling cloths and lying in a manger." 13 And suddenly there was with the angel a multitude of the heavenly host praising God and saying,

14 "Glory to God in the highest,
and on earth peace among men with whom he is pleased!"[a]

15 When the angels went away from them into heaven, the shepherds said to one another, "Let us go over to Bethlehem and see this thing that has happened, which the Lord has made known to us." 16 And they went with haste, and found Mary and Joseph, and the babe lying in a manger. 17 And when they saw it they made known the saying which had been told them concerning this child; 18 and all who heard it wondered at what the shepherds told them. 19 But Mary kept all these things, pondering them in her heart. 20 And the shepherds returned, glorifying and praising God for all they had heard and seen, as it had been told them.

10.

=====

In Luke 2, we learn about "The Boy Jesus in the Temple."

41 Now his parents went to Jerusalem every year at the feast of the Passover. 42 And when he was twelve years old, they went up according to custom; 43 and when the feast was ended, as they were returning, the boy Jesus stayed behind in Jerusalem. His parents did not know it, 44 but supposing him to be in the company they went a day's journey, and they sought him among their kinsfolk and acquaintances; 45 and when they did not find him, they returned to Jerusalem, seeking him. 46 After three days they found him in the temple, sitting among the teachers, listening to them and asking them questions; 47 and all who heard him were amazed at his understanding and his answers. 48 And when they saw him they were astonished; and his mother said to him, "Son, why have you treated us so? Behold, your father and I have been looking for you anxiously." 49 And he said to them, "How is it that you sought me? Did you not know that I must be in my Father's house?" 50 And they did not understand the saying which he spoke to them. 51 And he went down with them and came to Nazareth, and was obedient to them; and his mother kept all these things in her heart.

52 And Jesus increased in wisdom and in stature,[c] and in favor with God and man.

11.
=====

In Luke 12, Jesus gives "A Warning against Hypocrisy."

12 In the meantime, when so many thousands of the multitude had gathered together that they trod upon one another, he began to say to his disciples first, "Beware of the leaven of the Pharisees, which is hypocrisy. 2 Nothing is covered up that will not be revealed, or hidden that will not be known. 3 Therefore whatever you have said in the dark shall be heard in the light, and what you have whispered in private rooms shall be proclaimed upon the housetops.

(b) Lessons on Greatness from the Acts of the Apostles: Notes

Too many lessons to cite.

(c) **Lessons on Greatness from the Letters: Notes**

Too many lessons to cite.

(d) **Lessons on Greatness from the Revelation to John: Notes**

Too many lessons to cite.

========================

(7)

EPILOGUE

THEOSIS

========================

(a) **Introduction**

(i) Chapter Aim

The five popular paths to happiness are money, sex, power, fame, and greatness. God and the world have different views on these five paths. A faithful Christian who applies God's lessons - as taught by our Lord and Savior Jesus Christ - to him or herself will be rewarded with an abundant life and an elevated spiritual existence. Applying the Christian lessons revealed in the previous chapters of this book will lead to theosis, which is when a person becomes a god - through likeness to and union with God - attaining one's fullest divine potential. Biology teaches us that we are animals, but God reassures us that we can become divine. Theosis is not fiction. It is theology. It is living your best life.

Theosis is the lesser known Orthodox Christian path to happiness. This chapter is specifically on the nature of theosis and is a framework of the doctrine of theosis. In this chapter, I highlight the key elements of theosis and provide the formula for theosis. If you apply this chapter (and book) to yourself and make it a part of your lifestyle, you will be on the path to theosis and become a god. Theosis means being at our best and thereby attaining all the good qualities that come with it - including peace and happiness. With theosis, a person will acquire both peace and happiness to the fullest measure a person can in this world.

I must give much credit for this chapter to Norman Russell, specifically his work - *The Doctrine of Deification in the Greek Patristic Tradition* (2004), which is a scholarly 418-page volume published by Oxford University Press. I organized the layout of this chapter, gathered the chapter's content and added insight, but I learned much about deification from Russell. As I crafted this chapter, Russell's book was a vital resource. This chapter is a comprehensive summary of all aspects of deification (the English term for the Greek term "theosis") with the help of Russell and the Greek Church Fathers.

Some Church Fathers emphasized certain aspects of theosis more than other aspects, and as the years moved forward, each Church Father contributed what he learned to be true to the doctrine of theosis. In the doctrine, the theology works together, and the Church Fathers share many truths.

My aim has been to give a good general assessment of theosis with as simple a method and language that I can for my target audience - who is my neighbor and not the professional theologian. Professional theologians can enjoy this chapter, as well, but they should also go to Norman Russell who has done the great work in his masterful book.

As the saying goes, I have been able to see as far as I have because I have stood on the shoulders of giants. Russell is a giant to me, and I am certain he would agree that the Church Fathers are giants. I credit my knowledge to these giants who are my teachers. I am simply a student of these men, and my intention is to teach my neighbor what I have learned from these men about theosis.

(ii) Defining Theosis

In the English language, the three most common words that we see for God-likeness or when a person is becoming a god are… deification (becoming a deity), divinization (becoming divine), and theosis (in Greek, becoming a god). These words are predominantly used with the Eastern Church. In the Western Churches, theosis is "equivalent [to] … sanctifying grace" (Russell, 5).

In this chapter, I will provide answers to the following questions: Who are the gods in the Jewish and Christian Scriptures? What does it mean to be a god? How does a person become a god? What is the difference between God and a god? Theosis is the ultimate purpose of life and the ultimate goal of life for Christians. Theosis occurs on the way to God when a person has developed a strong and tight relationship with God.

The first person to give a formal definition for theosis was Dionysius the Areopagite in his *Ecclesiastical Hierarchy* where he declares, "Theosis is the attaining of likeness to God and union with him so far as is possible" (Russell, 1, 261).

(iii) Theosis Before Jesus Christ

The concept of theosis before Jesus Christ can be found in multiple sources - which come from the Jewish tradition, from philosophical religion in the Hellenistic tradition, and from other traditions around the world.

From the Jewish Tradition

The Jewish Scriptures have multiple references to gods that are origins for the Christian doctrine of theosis. As referenced in the Gospel According to John by our Lord and Savior Jesus Christ, Psalm 82 (specifically verses 1 and 6) (RSV) refers to gods and theosis:

> A Plea for Justice
> A Psalm of Asaph.
>
> 82 God has taken his place in the divine council;
>   in the midst of the gods he holds judgment:
> 2 "How long will you judge unjustly
>   and show partiality to the wicked? Selah
> 3 Give justice to the weak and the fatherless;
>   maintain the right of the afflicted and the destitute.

> 4 Rescue the weak and the needy;
>   deliver them from the hand of the wicked."
> 5 They have neither knowledge nor understanding,
>   they walk about in darkness;
>   all the foundations of the earth are shaken.
> 6 I say, "You are gods,
>   sons of the Most High, all of you;
> 7 nevertheless, you shall die like men,
>   and fall like any prince."[a]
> 8 Arise, O God, judge the earth;
>   for to thee belong all the nations!

Soon, I will explain how we can become "gods, sons of the Most High" (Psalm 82:6). Nevertheless, we cannot escape our humanity because we "shall die like men, and fall like any prince" (Psalm 82:7). With Jesus Christ, we can attain theosis and become gods, but as Jesus died, we, too, will die (Russell, 217). We can attain theosis - we can become gods - but we are still limited by the body in this life. If we are gifted with theosis, we will be on the path to God's Kingdom of Heaven and Eternal Life. It is in the afterlife and Resurrection where a person's theosis is fully realized and complete as a god. If we are blessed to enter God's Kingdom of Heaven and with Eternal Life, we become a part of "the divine council," where "God has taken his place" and where "in the midst of the gods he holds judgment" (82:1). In this chapter, I will reveal the elements of, the framework of, and the formula for theosis to illustrate how a person can attain theosis.

There are additional references to theosis in the Jewish Scriptures. For example, in Genesis 2 and 3, we learn that at the beginning, in Paradise, Adam and Eve were created for a divine destiny. They enjoyed immortality and contemplation of God. However, they fell from God's grace by sinning when they disobeyed God's command to not eat from the tree of knowledge. They listened to the serpent who "said to the woman, 'You will not die. 5 For God knows that when you eat of it your eyes will be opened, and you will be like God, knowing good and evil'" (Genesis 3:4-5). They misused their free will through attempting to grasp divinity on their own contrary to God's command by eating from the tree of knowledge. In the Fall, they lost divinity and acquired mortality, which was inherited by their descendants - all of humankind. According to Christianity, God redeemed humankind when God became a man, and so humankind regained its divine destiny, and as God planned, humankind is able to enjoy a more secure incorruption and more intimate closeness with God (Russell, 187, 221, 322).

In the Old Testament, Moses and other holy men are called sons of God and gods. In Scripture, Moses is said to be God-like. In Exodus 7:1 (RSV), it states, "And the Lord said to Moses, 'See, I make you as God to Pharaoh.'" We must climb up our mountains and emulate Moses who climbed up

Mount Sinai to behold God, so we, too, can be filled with divine glory (Russell, 75, 260).

The designation "god" is also seen in Deuteronomy 10:17 (RSV), as a part of "The Essence of the Law," where we learn: "For the Lord your God is God of gods and Lord of lords, the great, the mighty, and the terrible God, who is not partial and takes no bribe."

In Daniel 2:47 (RSV), it states: "The king said to Daniel, "Truly, your God is God of gods and Lord of kings, and a revealer of mysteries, for you have been able to reveal this mystery."

Psalm 136:2 (RSV) also references gods and theosis. There it states: "O give thanks to the God of gods, / for his steadfast love endures for ever."

Jesus understood these Old Testament references and declared that He is God's Son (Psalm 2). Athanasius taught that Jesus Christ, as the Eternal Word of God, pre-existed the sons of God and gods of the Old Testament and that He made possible their divine status. Christ is the Son of God by nature while the sons of God and gods of the Old Testament are so by adoption (Russell, 170).

References to immortality and "gods" were investigated and elaborated by the Jews of Hellenistic Judaism such as Philo of Alexandria, by the Jews of Enochic Judaism, and by the Jews of Rabbinic Judaism (Russell, 10-11).

Russell points out that the Judaism of Enoch contributed to the Christian doctrine of theosis with three visual images: (1) the gifted seer beholding the awesome throne-chariot of God, (2) the righteous dead sharing in the divine life and clothed with the radiant garments of glory, (3) the elect becoming like the angels by worshiping and serving God in His immediate Presence (Russell, 77).

In Ancient Israel, the Jewish spiritual life promoted the angelification of people as the way to theosis - because angels were recognized as the gods in Scripture (Russell, 53). In Rabbinic Judaism, observance of the Torah and obedience to the Law leads to immortality and angelic life; while disobedience leads to death (Russell, 73). God created Adam and Eve to be like the angels - if not superior to the angels - but Adam and Eve fell by sinfully disobeying God. Observance of the Torah reverses the punishment of the Fall and returns a person to God-like angelic theosis (Russell, 74). The heroic Moses ascended up Mount Sinai and became like an angel. When he descended with the Law of God, he was a god leading people to God and to theosis. He was the forerunner of a new humanity (Russell, 75).

From Philosophical Religion in the Hellenistic Tradition

The doctrine of theosis also has influences from philosophical religion found in the Hellenistic tradition - particularly from the works of Plato, Aristotle, Plotinus, and some Stoic philosophy. The role of Greek philosophy on the Church doctrine of theosis is relevant and important. Greek thought is responsible for the philosophical approach to theosis (Russell, 14-15). Platonic philosophy teaches that theosis is attainment of likeness to God. Platonism teaches that likeness to God is the goal and end of spiritual life (Russell, 35). It also encourages participation with the divine, uses the metaphor of the soul's ascent, and promotes reaching out to God in ecstasy (Russell, 52).

As Russell points out, Clement of Alexandria - who was influenced by Platonism - explained that the Christian philosopher on the path of theosis practices likeness to and assimilation to God as the goal of human life. This means living according to virtue and righteousness, with self-restraint, with endurance, by ruling over the passions, by sharing his possessions, and by doing good. Like God, the Christian philosopher must be free from passion, be self-sufficient, and be beneficent. Like God, he must rule like a king. This includes ruling like a king over the wild beasts in his exterior world as well as ruling like a king over the passions in his interior world (Russell, 134-135).

Greek Philosopher Plotinus believed we are meant to return to the Source, and this is done by turning inwards. With our souls, divinity is already in us. We must purify our souls and attain the good, which is found most perfectly above in the divine realm. Our souls are of the same substance as the World Soul and the Divine Source. The goal is to become one with the Divine Source, yet we are not absorbed into It as taught by Eastern Philosophy (namely Hinduism, specifically in the teaching of Moksha). When a person reaches union with the Divine, the result is ecstasy (Russell, 40-41).

Greek philosophy added value in the development of the doctrine of theosis. Greek philosophy nourished the blossoming of the doctrine of theosis. Greek philosophy was necessary for the fullness of the doctrine of theosis. Its influence was instrumental to the maturity of the doctrine. Greek philosophy should not be put at odds with the Bible, and it should not be regarded as inherently corrupt. Greek philosophy speaks truths and therefore is not alien to Biblical Truth. Plato himself - through philosophy - was first to identify the four cardinal virtues (prudence, justice, fortitude, temperance), which appear later, as well, in the Christian Apocrypha (Wisdom of Solomon 8:7 and 4 Maccabees 1:18-19) and then Christian theologians, such as Saint Augustine, confirmed them and added to them the three theological virtues (faith, hope, love).

In Exodus 12:35-36, it states: "35 The people of Israel had also done as Moses told them, for they had asked of the Egyptians jewelry of silver and of gold, and clothing; 36 and the Lord had given the people favor in the sight of the Egyptians, so that they let them have what they asked. Thus they despoiled the Egyptians." Christian Theologian Origen applied this lesson in Scripture to Christian theology. Thomas Guarino notes how "Origen argued that the Church, like the ancient Israelites, had been licensed to 'despoil the Egyptians,' using their philosophical 'gold' for the glory of God" (Guarino, *The Unchanging Truth of God?*, 19). Just as Israel was encouraged to use Egyptian gold, the Church is encouraged to use ideas outside the Bible, such as Greek philosophy, for the glory of God. Greek philosophy can be useful. Western Philosophy has value, as does Eastern Philosophy, such as Hinduism, Taoism, and Buddhism. They all have truths to teach, though the highest truths are found in Christianity.

Russell points out that Hellenists contributed to the Christian doctrine of theosis with four philosophical teachings: (1) immortality is a gift from God, not to be attributed to the individual, (2) the human soul is divine, yet God is, nevertheless, beyond us, (3) through moral progress, the human soul can participate in divine attributes, (4) the human mind has the potential even in this life to attain an ecstatic encounter with God (Russell, 77).

From Other Traditions Around the World

As Russell notes, there was an idea of theosis in the Greco-Roman World that was outside Jewish theology and Hellenistic philosophy with the Ruler-Cult, the Mystery Cults, and the Egyptian Hermetists.

In addition, throughout the world, heroic cults that became divine cults were popular. These cults followed extraordinary men and women when they were alive and worshiped them after death as gods. For example, in South Asia around 500 BC, Siddhartha Gautama, who is the historical Buddha (meaning Enlightened One or Awakened One) - with his virtuous and sanctifying qualities - has been honored as divine. In Greece, around the same time, Pythagoras, who was a philosopher and shamanistic wonder worker, was also seen as a divine man. In the Roman Empire, emperors - such as Julius Caesar - were considered divine and were worshiped in cults.

What sets Jesus Christ apart from all other people who gathered followers is that while other groups faded in time, Jesus' following has passed the test of time and continues to thrive. While cults have come and gone, Christianity has remained and even grown since it emerged 2,000 years ago. The success of Jesus' following can be attributed to three factors: (1) Jesus' divine presence and power still live supernaturally in the world affirming that He is the Living God; (2) Jesus is the only person who fulfills Jewish prophecy of God's Chosen One - as expressed in the Hebrew Scriptures, like the book of Isaiah - and this fulfillment of prophecy must not be ignored because it serves as evidence that He is the One; (3) Jesus' historical and physical Resurrection from the dead - as attested by His tortured and martyred Apostles - confirms that He is God.

(iv) Theosis and Jesus Christ

In the Gospel According to John 10:34-38, we learn how Jesus Christ understood theosis, applied the theology of theosis to Himself, and used the theology to teach the world. Below is Jesus' reference to theosis in John 10 (RSV):

> 22 It was the feast of the Dedication at Jerusalem; 23 it was winter, and Jesus was walking in the temple, in the portico of Solomon. 24 So the Jews gathered round him and said to him, "How long will you keep us

in suspense? If you are the Christ, tell us plainly." 25 Jesus answered them, "I told you, and you do not believe. The works that I do in my Father's name, they bear witness to me; 26 but you do not believe, because you do not belong to my sheep. 27 My sheep hear my voice, and I know them, and they follow me; 28 and I give them eternal life, and they shall never perish, and no one shall snatch them out of my hand. 29 My Father, who has given them to me,[a] is greater than all, and no one is able to snatch them out of the Father's hand. 30 I and the Father are one."

31 The Jews took up stones again to stone him. 32 Jesus answered them, "I have shown you many good works from the Father; for which of these do you stone me?" 33 The Jews answered him, "It is not for a good work that we stone you but for blasphemy; because you, being a man, make yourself God." 34 Jesus answered them, "Is it not written in your law, 'I said, you are gods'? 35 If he called them gods to whom the word of God came (and scripture cannot be broken), 36 do you say of him whom the Father consecrated and sent into the world, 'You are blaspheming,' because I said, 'I am the Son of God'? 37 If I am not doing the works of my Father, then do not believe me; 38 but if I do them, even though you do not believe me, believe the

works, that you may know and understand that the Father is in me and I am in the Father." 39 Again they tried to arrest him, but he escaped from their hands.

40 He went away again across the Jordan to the place where John at first baptized, and there he remained. 41 And many came to him; and they said, "John did no sign, but everything that John said about this man was true." 42 And many believed in him there.

As I mentioned earlier, Jesus' reference here in the Gospel According to John regarding God's Will for us to be gods is from the Jewish Scriptures, specifically Psalm 82:6.

(b) **Christian Doctrine of Theosis**

Those with theosis have received God's Word and have God's Word dwelling in them. This includes the Jewish Patriarchs, the Jewish Prophets, and all the Holy People of the Bible - as well as all the Christian Saints who study and live by God's Word. Christ is the Incarnation of God's Word and makes theosis possible for humankind. Theosis is a divine gift from God and is not a natural quality of a human being.

(i) In the New Testament

Jesus

As previously cited from the Gospel According to John 10:34b-38 (RSV), Jesus explained to His detractors:

> "Is it not written in your law, 'I said, you are gods'? 35 If he called them gods to whom the word of God came (and scripture cannot be broken), 36 do you say of him whom the Father consecrated and sent into the world, 'You are blaspheming,' because I said, 'I am the Son of God'? 37 If I am not doing the works of my Father, then do not believe me; 38 but if I do them, even though you do not believe me, believe the works, that you may know and understand that the Father is in me and I am in the Father."

After Jesus, major Christian theologians contributed to the development and maturity of the doctrine of theosis, which, as I have said, is when a person becomes a god - through likeness to and union with God - attaining one's fullest divine potential. A fundamental truth for Christians is that Jesus Christ - as God the Son - is God enfleshed, and so for a person to attain union with God, one must be united with Christ.

Paul

A key component to Paul's theology of theosis is participatory union with and in Christ. In 1 Corinthians 15 (RSV), Paul explains: "22 For as in Adam all die, so also in Christ shall all be made alive." From Paul, we are taught that participatory union in Christ is to be truly alive, and theosis is true life.

In 1 Corinthians 15 (RSV), Paul also explains: "45 Thus it is written, "The first man Adam became a living being"; the last Adam became a life-giving spirit. 46 But it is not the spiritual which is first but the physical, and then the spiritual. 47 The first man was from the earth, a man of dust; the second man is from heaven. 48 As was the man of dust, so are those who are of the dust; and as is the man of heaven, so are those who are of heaven. 49 Just as we have borne the image of the man of dust, we shall[b] also bear the image of the man of heaven. 50 I tell you this, brethren: flesh and blood cannot inherit the kingdom of God, nor does the perishable inherit the imperishable." In this passage from Paul, we learn that the "last Adam," the "second man," the "man of heaven" is our Lord and Savior Jesus Christ, who blesses His most faithful followers with heavenly theosis.

In 2 Corinthians 5 (RSV), Paul teaches: "17 Therefore, if any one is in Christ, he is a new creation;[a] the old has passed away, behold, the new has come." This new creation of a person is a person with theosis.

In Galatians 2:20b (RSV), Paul declares: "it is no longer I who live, but Christ who lives in me." The divinity of Christ lives in all faithful Christians making them divine. Participatory union with and in Christ was important to Paul and to the Christian doctrine of theosis.

John

Like the Letters of Paul, the Gospel According to John and the Letters of John teach that participatory union with and in Christ - the Life and Light of men - leads to divine life, which is theosis.

John 1 (RSV) begins by announcing that "The Word Became Flesh." This sublime preamble proclaims the Divinity of the Word of God - Who is our Lord and Savior Jesus Christ:

> 1 In the beginning was the Word, and the Word was with God, and the Word was God. 2 He was in the beginning with God; 3 all things were made through him, and without him was not anything made that was made. 4 In him was life,[a] and the life was the light of men. 5 The light shines in the darkness, and the darkness has not overcome it.
>
> 6 There was a man sent from God, whose name was John. 7 He came for testimony, to bear witness to the light, that all might believe through him. 8 He was not the light, but came to bear witness to the light.
>
> 9 The true light that enlightens every man was coming into the world. 10 He was in the world, and the world was made through him, yet the world knew him not. 11 He came to his own home, and his own people received him not. 12 But to all who received him, who

believed in his name, he gave power to become children of God; 13 who were born, not of blood nor of the will of the flesh nor of the will of man, but of God.

14 And the Word became flesh and dwelt among us, full of grace and truth; we have beheld his glory, glory as of the only Son from the Father. 15 (John bore witness to him, and cried, "This was he of whom I said, 'He who comes after me ranks before me, for he was before me.'") 16 And from his fulness have we all received, grace upon grace. 17 For the law was given through Moses; grace and truth came through Jesus Christ. 18 No one has ever seen God; the only Son,[b] who is in the bosom of the Father, he has made him known.

Most significant for our study on theosis at this moment is when John says, "12 But to all who received him, who believed in his name, he gave power to become children of God; 13 who were born, not of blood nor of the will of the flesh nor of the will of man, but of God." The children of God who are born of God are gods, and thus have theosis.

Peter

From Peter's teachings, in the Second Letter of Peter 1 (RSV), we learn, "3 His divine power has granted to us all things that pertain to life and godliness, through the knowledge of him who called us to[c] his own glory and excellence, 4 by which he has granted to us his precious and very great promises, that through these you may escape from the corruption that is in the world because of passion, and become partakers of the divine nature." These two verses are key to understanding theosis. "[D]ivine power has granted" to the elect "life and godliness," which is theosis. "[K]noweldge" of God and Christ leads to God's "glory and excellence," which is theosis. "[H]is precious and very great promises" include theosis. "[E]scape from the corruption that is in the world" is a fruit of theosis. And, lastly, and, perhaps, most importantly, when the elect "become partakers of the divine nature," they possess theosis. "Partakers of the divine nature" participate with God and His attributes and in His spiritual gifts, such as the Church Sacraments. By partaking of the divine nature, we become divine and are blessed with theosis.

James

From James's teachings, in the Letter of James 1 (RSV), we learn: "17 Every good endowment and every perfect gift is from above, coming down from the Father of lights..." The gift of theosis comes down to us from God, and we must apply this gift to ourselves in order to return to Him. Theosis is about returning to the Source of light, love, and life. As Russell notes, Dionysus the Areopagite began his *Celestial Hierarchy* - his treatise on angelic theosis - with this verse from James 1 (Russell, 250).

(ii) After the New Testament

In *The Doctrine of Deification in the Greek Patristic Tradition*, Russell investigates the works of the major Christian theologians who reveal the nature of deification (theosis).

After identifying the New Testament authors who delve into the theology of theosis and examining their writings, Russell continues with the Fathers of the early Church. Next, he teaches us about the doctrine of theosis from Alexandrian Christianity. Then, we are introduced to the Cappadocian Christian Fathers and their approach to theosis. After, we are taught about the Christian Monastic Synthesis of theosis. This is followed by later developments to the doctrine of theosis and the modern approaches to theosis. In Appendix 1, Russell also adds the theology of theosis in the Syriac and Latin Traditions.

With the theologians of these schools of thought, the theology of theosis grew and was expressed with greater clarity over the centuries. References from the Church Fathers will appear in this chapter as I continue to elaborate on the elements of, the framework of, and the formula for theosis.

(c) **Role of God as Holy Trinity**

God is the Source of theosis. He is the Source of goodness though He is beyond all good qualities and gifts. In my book *Beholding Heavenly Light: Lessons from Christian Masterpieces*, I explain how the Eastern Church encourages us to describe Almighty God…

> the mode of expression or articulation applied to our Transcendent God that is more appropriate is in negative theological terms rather than in positive terms (this is also known as the apophatic approach) because no

description can fully represent God since He is Invisible (Not-Visible), Infinite (Not-Finite) and Unbound (Not-Bound). This mode of expression provides insight in the way we should read Scripture to imagine the mysterious nature of the transcendent...

(Angelidis, 67)

God is a Holy Trinity - a Being with three coequal, coeternal, consubstantial Divine Persons Who freely engage in communal love as One. Evidence of Holy Trinity theology (Almighty God as Father, Son, and Holy Spirit) in the Old Testament clearly appears in Isaiah 9:6 (RSV),

> 6 For to us a child is born,
>   to us a son is given;
> and the government will be upon his shoulder,
>   and his name will be called
> "Wonderful Counselor [Holy Spirit], Mighty God,
>   Everlasting Father [Father], Prince of Peace [Son]."

The Holy Trinity lives within Jesus Christ (the child born, the son given). The Holy Trinity is Jewish theology that Jesus Christ elaborated on and the Christian Church crystalized in doctrine.

(i) God the Father

With the Divine Inspiration of the Holy Spirit, the Church Father's carefully crafted the Nicene Creed, which begins with the Christian belief about God the Father. Regarding God the Father, the Church Fathers taught us to say:

> I believe in one God, Father Almighty, Creator of heaven and earth, and of all things visible and invisible.
>
> (www.goarch.org/-/the-nicene-creed. Accessed 5-10-2023)

When God created humankind, God identified Himself with "us" and "our," which the Church Fathers believed indicate God's nature as Holy Trinity. God also made humankind in His image and after His likeness. In Genesis 1 (RSV), it says:

> 26 Then God said, "Let us make man in our image, after our likeness; and let them have dominion over the fish of the sea, and over the birds of the air, and over the cattle, and over

all the earth, and over every creeping thing that creeps upon the earth." 27 So God created man in his own image, in the image of God he created him; male and female he created them.

Here, we are taught that God made human beings in His image and after His likeness. Theologians such as Clement of Alexandria (Russell, 135), Diadochus of Photice (Russell, 246-247), and John Damascene (Russell, 299) have distinguished between "image" and "likeness." As human beings, Adam and Eve were made by God in His image. This image refers to God's spiritual qualities. God is Spirit (Genesis 1:2, John 4:24), and human beings were made as spiritual beings. Image refers to spiritual nature. Some theologians, like those just mentioned, believe likeness is different. Human beings were originally also made after God's likeness. Human beings' likeness to God was corrupted by the Fall. When Eve and Adam disobeyed God's commands, humanity fell and lost its likeness to God. After the Fall, Adam and Eve remained in the image of God, but lost God's likeness, which refers to God's virtuous qualities. Because of their disobedience, Adam and Eve lost virtue. Likeness refers to virtue. Today, to become a god, a person - who is born with a God-like spiritual image - must regain his or her God-like virtuous likeness. Acquiring and developing virtue and virtuous qualities is one aspect of attaining theosis - becoming a god - and of regaining the intended divine state that God destined for us despite the Fall. We must cultivate in ourselves God's likeness through keeping His commandments and growing in virtue to attain theosis, to become a god. Basil of Caesarea believed in this approach of cultivating virtue to attain theosis (Russell, 208, 211).

The goal of theosis for human beings is possible by recovering divine likeness and attaining union with God so far as a human being can. God's Incarnation in the person of Jesus Christ makes theosis possible. Almighty God makes those in whom He dwells into gods.

(ii) God the Son

The Nicene Creed begins with God the Father and continues with God the Son. Regarding God the Son, the Church Fathers taught us to say:

> And [I believe] in one Lord Jesus Christ, the only-begotten Son of God, begotten of the Father before all ages; Light of Light, true God of true God, begotten, not created, of one essence with the Father through Whom all things were made. Who for us men and for our

salvation came down from heaven and was incarnate of the Holy Spirit and the Virgin Mary and became man. He was crucified for us under Pontius Pilate, and suffered and was buried; And He rose on the third day, according to the Scriptures. He ascended into heaven and is seated at the right hand of the Father; And He will come again with glory to judge the living and dead. His kingdom shall have no end.

(www.goarch.org/-/the-nicene-creed. Accessed 5-10-2023)

The Son is the Incarnation of God. God condescended Himself and took on flesh without losing any degree of His Divinity. He did not resign His Divinity by becoming a man. He accepted the weakness of a man - without that weakness changing His Divine Nature (Russell, 327).

God took on human nature as one of us when he was born in Bethlehem. He was given the name Jesus, which in Hebrew means "God Saves." Jesus is God. Jesus identified Himself as God Eternal when He said, "Truly, truly, I say to you, before Abraham was, I am" (John 8:58, RSV). Still further, with this "I am" statement, Jesus was directly referencing God who declared to Moses, "I AM WHO I AM." […] "Say this to the people of Israel, 'I AM has sent me to you.'" (Exodus 3:13-3:15, RSV). By applying God's

"I AM" declaration from the Hebrew Scriptures to Himself, Jesus identified Himself as God. Jesus applied the Hebrew Scriptures to Himself often to announce His Divinity. Jesus is also Savior. He was a perfect man without sin who was born to "save his people from their sins." (Matthew 1:21, RSV). He has the power to save us in this fallen world from corruption, sin, death, and hell.

God enfleshed, Jesus was one person with two natures - fully divine and fully human - united together. The Incarnation is the union of God and man, the union of heavenly and earthly. God became Incarnate to return, restore, and unite fallen human beings with Himself. God descended to human beings, so human beings can ascend to God. The purpose was to transform fallen humanity and elevate human beings into divinity.

God became a man, so man can become a god. This is the "exchange formula," which was first formally articulated by Irenaeus of Lyons (Russell, 106) when he said that God the Son "became what we are in order to make us what he is himself" (*Against Heresies*, Book V, "Preface"). The exchange formula has roots in Paul's thinking (Russell, 108), and it continues to reappear with subsequent theologians, such as Athanasius who adopted the formula and further affirmed, promoted, and popularized it in his writings (Russell, 169). Maximus the Confessor elaborated and expanded on it, as well (Russell, 262).

The exchange formula is perhaps the most celebrated and influential theology in the doctrine of theosis.

God was enfleshed for the theosis of man. God took on flesh and thereby brought theosis to flesh. He became Incarnate for man's theosis. Just as a teacher transforms his student with the knowledge he imparts, as a master carpenter makes his apprentice a carpenter or, as Clement of Alexandria said, Plato makes his disciples into philosophers, so, too, God educates human beings and transforms mortals into immortals and thereby gods (Russell, 126).

Jesus Christ is the New Adam. Christ's obedience to God mends the rift of Adam and Eve's disobedience to God. Christ succeeded where Adam and Eve failed. Christ is the new Adam who gives us a fresh start. He reverses and undoes the damage done by Adam. As the New Adam, He makes possible a second birth. Christ heals our fallen wounded souls and restores our relationship with God. Irenaeus of Lyons taught that "The New Creation in Christ 'Recapitulates' the Old" (Richardson, *Early Christian Fathers*, 333). This recapitulation - recapping - of Adam by Jesus not only makes possible the return of humankind's divinity that Adam originally enjoyed; it also makes possible for each of us to reach his or her fullest divine potential that is superior to what Adam and Eve enjoyed and that is Christ-like (Russell, 221). As believers of Christ, we gain a Christ-like divine existence. We can be confident in this transformation because of Christ's Resurrection, which prefigures our Resurrection. Theologians, such as Justin Martyr, contend that theosis is no longer attained strictly through obedience to the Jewish Torah, but is now possible through obedience to Christ's commandments (Russell, 101).

Jesus Christ is our Mediator. Christ was unique as fully God and fully human united perfectly in one person. In His unique role, Christ is the Mediator between God and man. He is the Bridge between the Uncreated and created, between heaven and earth. He gives us access to eternal life.

Only God is immortal and incorrupt; however, human beings can participate with these divine attributes of God if we unite ourselves to God the Son. Christian Theologian Origen maintained that Christ alone is wise, righteous, and rational. People are lost because of sin and are only wise, righteous, and rational through imitating Christ and sharing in His attributes. Christ is the Light of God, and people possess light only through participating in Christ. Only with Christ can people participate in the Father, who is the Source of everything of the Son. The Son is a power who deifies and enlightens. He gives us the Life and Light of the Father (Russell, 150).

Christ - as God the Son of the Holy Trinity - is the agent of redemption and theosis. Christ makes His faithful followers into christs.

(iii) God the Holy Spirit

After identifying God the Father and God the Son in the Nicene Creed, the Church Fathers identify God the Holy Spirit. Regarding God the Holy Spirit, the Church Fathers taught us to say:

> And [I believe] in the Holy Spirit, the Lord, the Creator of life, Who proceeds from the Father, Who together with the Father and the Son is worshipped and glorified, Who spoke through the prophets.
>
> (www.goarch.org/-/the-nicene-creed. Accessed 5-10-2023)

When analyzing Cyril of Alexandria's theology, Russell explains, "The Son's work of salvation is carried out through the Spirit" (Russell, 200). The Holy Spirit leads us to Baptism, inaugurates us during Baptism, and gives us life after Baptism. We partake of the Spirit in Baptism. The Holy Spirit transforms a person. Cyril taught - like Paul before him - that our bodies are meant to be temples of the Holy Spirit, and if the Holy Spirit is in us, then God is in us, and we become gods. The Holy Spirit compels us to cry out to God and call Him Father. The Spirit renews a person daily. He is the Giver of holy gifts. He perfects, beatifies, sanctifies, deifies, and makes human beings spiritual. The Holy Spirit fills the saints and makes them into gods. We must participate in the Spirit's Holiness. The Holy Spirit dwells in those who keep God's commandments and who live faithful devout lives. The Holy Spirit has the power to sanctify - to change an earthly man into a heavenly man. He mingles with people's souls and transforms people into saints. The saints reciprocate the love of the Holy Spirit. The saints answer the heavenly call and participate with and in the Holy Spirit, the only-begotten Son, and the Heavenly Father.

One of the most sublime prayers in Eastern Orthodox Christianity is directed to the Holy Spirit. It appears as a part of the Trisagion Prayers, which many Orthodox Christians use daily. It says:

> O heavenly King, O Comforter, the Spirit of truth, who art in all places and fillest all things; Treasury of good things and Giver of life: Come and dwell in us and cleanse us from every stain, and save our souls, O gracious Lord.

(Antiochian Orthodox Christian Archdiocese of North America, *A Pocket Prayer Book for Orthodox Christians*, 5)

The Holy Spirit gives the saints holy spirits. We must gradually become more spiritual and live by the Holy Spirit. The gifts of the Holy Spirit dwelling within a person are faith, hope, and love.

I can testify that when the Holy Spirit fills my soul, I am as happy as I can be. Nothing is better. Life feels like a dream, but it is better than a dream because it is a living reality. It is similar to the power of inspiration, but this heavenly ecstasy lasts longer, is deeper, and is more profound than the boost of inspiration. I have had many moments where I have not slept for days, but have nonetheless had energy, vitality, vigor, and happiness. This does not happen often, but it happens often enough that I am aware of the Holy Spirit's presence in me. It is beautiful, beatific, and divine. And, this experience - as I have read and learned - is only a glimpse, hint, and taste of the life, love, light, joy, happiness that we will experience in Eternity with God the Father, God the Son, God the Holy Spirit, the Most Holy Virgin Mother Mary, the Angels, and the Saints. Knowledge of this Holy Spirit experience itself is mystifying and delivers enough fuel on the journey of life that lasts to the next destination. I live for these pure moments and look forward to them in uninterrupted perfection and completion in Paradise.

* * *

God exists as a Holy Trinity and desires our Salvation and theosis. From the Father - the Son and the Holy Spirit deify one's soul, and one's soul has the power to deify the person. When expounding the theology of Athanasius, Russell points out, "Deification [theosis] is a work of the Son in conjunction with the Spirit" (Russell, 175). By partaking of the Son and the Spirit, we partake in the Father because both come from the Father and are of one essence with the Father. Russell brings to our attention how Athanasius maintained that adoption, renewal, salvation, sanctification, grace, transcendence, illumination, and vivification are equivalent to theosis. As Russell explains, Athanasius believed that "[d]eification [theosis] is certainly liberation from death and corruption, but it is also adoption as sons, the renewal of our nature by participation in the divine nature, a sharing in the bond of love of the Father and the Son, and finally entry into the kingdom of heaven in the likeness of Christ" (Russell, 178). The saints experience ecstasy in theosis when their souls ascend to a mystical union with the Holy Trinity.

(d) Role of the Church Sacraments

The Church Sacraments are our means to the divine life and theosis. By participating in the Sacraments, we participate in the divine life. All Church Sacraments are important. The Sacraments were instituted by Christ and entrusted to the Church. They are blessings given to us by the Bridegroom Christ for His Bride the Church to prepare us for when the Bridegroom returns inaugurating a celebratory wedding banquet with the Bride. All the Sacraments are from Christ's exemplary life and teachings. They allow the believer to participate with Christ. They supernaturally raise the soul to God and prepare the body for Resurrection and Eternal Life. With regard to theosis, there are two Sacraments that are particularly important: Baptism and the Eucharist.

As Russell explores Gregory of Nazianzus's theology of theosis, Russell explains that the priest is an agent of theosis as he administers the Sacraments (Russell, 222). At Church services, especially the Divine Liturgy, the priest brings believers to theosis in the presence of God, the Most Holy Virgin Mother Mary, the Angels, and the Saints as the earthly and the heavenly commingle during the Church service. This helps the faithful rise to contemplate the divine and unite with God. The most significant Sacraments that a priest administers for theosis are Baptism and the Eucharist.

(i) Baptism

In the Bible's four Gospels (although, indirectly in the Gospel According to John), we learn about Jesus Christ's Baptism. Christ was Baptized by Saint John the Forerunner in the Jordan River and thereby gave us an example to follow. For each human being, Baptism is the beginning of theosis. It is the first step towards theosis. It is the beginning of a new life with Christ. Baptism is a rebirth. Baptism is a healing medicine that takes away sin. It is the bath of salvation, illumination, adoption, perfection, immortality.

Christ is the only-begotten Son of God who is coeternal with the Father. Through Baptism, we, too, can become sons of the Father - although, we become adopted sons of the Father. With grace, God the Father gave us His only-begotten Son to guide us and to make us adopted sons and to save us with eternal life. God adopts us so we can call Him Father. This is adoption by grace. Our adoption as sons and daughters into this Holy Family is made possible through Baptism.

Typically, in the Orthodox Church, during the Baptismal Sacrament, a priest immerses the initiate in blessed water three times in the name of the Father, the Son, and the Holy Spirit. The initiate descends into water and then ascends out of water and thereby correspondingly dies and rises with Christ. In Baptism, the initiate dies with Christ leaving behind sin and then rises into a new life with the Father, the Son, and the Holy Spirit. It is a rebirth, transformation, divine birth. In Baptism, we are united with the Holy Spirit and are deified with the Son and the Holy Spirit. The waters regenerate our spirit with the Holy Spirit. The blessed waters purify our bodies and souls to save us.

Baptism removes evil from us. It restores our relationship with God and spiritually renews us, so we can continue with our spiritual development. Baptism prepares the believer for the divine life and prepares the believer for future trials. Baptism allows and prepares the believer to take the Eucharist. Only with Baptism can a person receive the Eucharist.

(ii) The Eucharist

In the Bible's four Gospels, we learn about Jesus' Last Supper with His disciples. The Gospel According to Matthew 26 (RSV) reveals Jesus' extraordinary actions and words at the Last Supper:

> 26 Now as they were eating, Jesus took bread, and blessed, and broke it, and gave it to the disciples and said, "Take, eat; this is my body." 27 And he took a cup, and when he had given thanks he gave it to them, saying, "Drink of it, all of you; 28 for this is my blood of the[c] covenant, which is poured out for many for the forgiveness of sins. 29 I tell you I shall not drink again of this fruit of the vine until that day when I drink it new with you in my Father's kingdom."

And, the Gospel According to Luke 22 (RSV) explains:

> 19 And he took bread, and when he had given thanks he broke it and gave it to them, saying, "This is my body which is given for you. Do this in remembrance of me." 20 And likewise the cup after supper, saying, "This cup which is poured out for you is the new covenant in my blood."

Jesus said, "Do this in remembrance of me," and we follow our Lord's command every time we partake in the Eucharist. We honor and obey our Lord with the Sacrament of the Eucharist - where bread and wine become the Body and Blood of our Lord. We remember and thank Him for sacrificing His Body and Blood on the Cross. The Eucharist is truly the Body and Blood of Christ. The Lord did not say the bread and wine symbolize my body and blood. The Lord said "this is my body" and "this is my blood." Without confusion, we are receiving Jesus Christ.

  The Eucharist - also known as Holy Communion - is a mystery that transcends reason. It nurtures our theosis and nourishes the body and the soul. The Eucharist maintains our union with the Holy Spirit, which was initiated by Baptism. Cyril of Alexandria affirmed that the Eucharist "restores man wholly to incorruption" (Russell, 202). A gift from Christ, the Eucharist (from the Greek word eucharistia meaning "thanksgiving") is the Source of Life and leads to immortality of body and soul; and, therefore, It should not be neglected. "The Eucharist causes the passions to atrophy and dispels death and disease" (Russell, 202). It does not change us in a mechanical way and must be received with moral progress in participation with the Holy Spirit.

  From bread and wine into the Body and Blood of Christ, the Eucharist makes possible for believers to participate and commune with Christ. When receiving the Body and Blood of Jesus Christ, the

Christian partakes in and participates with Jesus Christ in both a physical sense and a spiritual sense. The Eucharist makes it possible for believers to unite with Christ's holy, immortal, and incorrupt nature (Russell, 228).

    The gift of the Eucharist allows us to participate with Christ, so we can be united to Him and attain theosis with Him. Through the Eucharist, we are united to Christ. He enters us and we become a member of Him. The Eucharist also unites individual participants together in Christ. God brings His people together when we congregate for the Eucharist and partake of the Eucharist. With the Eucharist and the loving relationship It stimulates, we are united with one another and God - in foresight of Heavenly Existence in Paradise.

    To be made acceptable for partaking in the Eucharist, we must prepare with ascetical fasting and, when necessary, be purified by Confession where a person confesses one's sins to one's spiritual father or parish priest. If we are prepared by fasting and purified by Confession, we will be ready to participate in the Eucharist, which will make us one with Christ.

    The Eucharist is the greatest and most sacred Sacramental gift offered by the Church. It is the central climatic moment of the Divine Liturgy. As with Baptism, the priest is an agent of theosis with the Eucharist (Russell, 222).

(e) **Role of the Human Being**

With love, God created human beings who are supposed to abide by God and love God in return. When Eve and Adam disobeyed God's command in the Garden of Eden, they exercised their free will. Their choice had repercussions that lead to the loss of their immortality and that lead to their mortality and death. Obeying God's commands leads to life, while disobeying God's commands leads to death. Theosis is life. Anyone can choose theosis because God gave His holy commandments to everyone. Theosis is not automatic and does not happen overnight and is rather a process toward progress. It begins by using our free will and choosing to follow God. It depends on spiritual growth, spiritual advancement, and spiritual maturity.

The opportunity for Salvation is in our response to God and His Christ. God does not use force on us to follow Him; He persuades us with love to join Him. He "callest all to salvation through the promise of blessings to come" (Antiochian Orthodox Christian Archdiocese of North America, *A Pocket Prayer Book for Orthodox Christians*, 11). With our free will, we must choose to live faithful lives. When this present harsh fallen world - influenced by the evil one - beats us down, the faithful know that only God and His Christ can save them. Those who choose Christ and abide in Christ are on the path of theosis.

God descended in the person of Jesus Christ and we must respond by ascending. We must reach up toward God, so we can be lifted up by Him. We must ascend with our souls just as Moses ascended Mount Sinai (Russell, 260). Because of our fallenness, we must look up and return to God. This leads to a higher unity and a more intimate relationship with God (Russell, 270).

Faith is an essential prerequisite for theosis. As we learn from the Gospel According to John 3:16 (RSV),

> For God so loved the world that he gave his only Son, that whoever believes in him should not perish but have eternal life.

This passage from John sums up the main message of the Gospels. It is related to Paul's theology of participatory union with Christ which leads to theosis, immortality, and eternal life.

It is also important to emphasize that theosis cannot be achieved in isolation without the social dimension of human nature. Jesus teaches us to love our neighbors as well as love our enemies. This love between human beings - to be brothers and sisters - is an important element in Jesus' teachings and exemplary life. Even so, alone independent time is important. Even Jesus needed time alone to pray to His Father. Many important functions of life are accomplished when we are away from others. However, the social aspect of human life cannot be ignored. The social dimension of human life is exemplified by the nature of God as Holy Trinity with each Divine Person working together ever harmoniously as One (Russell, 313). This is also illustrated by the various roles of the Church and how the different members make up One Body. Love is key to all healthy relationships in life as well as to the path of theosis.

It is critical to understand that even though human beings must choose to respond to God, theosis is not attributed to human effort but is initiated by God and is always a gift from God's grace. God created us as human beings by nature and desires to adopt us as His children - as gods - in spirit by grace. Even so, we must take steps toward Him to become His children and gods.

* * *

In addition to Baptism and receiving the Eucharist, there are three ways a person must respond to God to attain theosis: (1) through imitation of

God's virtuous attributes with agape love as the preeminent divine attribute; (2) through asceticism to gain dispassion - particularly from temptations of the flesh for bodily satisfaction - and to manage the struggle of life; and (3) through living a contemplative life to gain knowledge of God and to develop ceaseless prayer. When a person responds to God in these ways - Baptism, Eucharist, imitation, asceticism, contemplation - the person will maximize the potential to experience some level of theosis.

(i) Imitation of God

When I began my journey to wisdom, truth, and God at the age of 22, the most natural and the most basic approach to God for me was to embody good qualities like virtues and eliminate bad qualities like sins. I took this approach to imitate God because God is All Good with no negative qualities. This was one of the first methods I applied to myself when I began my journey to God. This is not a bad approach, if you are trying to reach God - the Greatest Good and Ultimate Goal.

However, to be clear, God Almighty is Uncreated, Timeless, Limitless, Infinite, Incomprehensible. As I mentioned earlier, this mode of expression or articulation applied to our Transcendent God is known as apophatic theology, which uses negative theological terms rather than positive terms because no description can fully represent God since He is Invisible (Not-Visible), Infinite (Not-Finite) and Unbound (Not-Bound). This method of referring to Almighty God is more appropriate because He is Indescribable - even though most people are accustomed to using positive terms to describe Almighty God (Angelidis, *Beholding Heavenly Light*, 67, 138). We will never share God's unapproachable essence, but we should cultivate in ourselves God's good qualities.

    Virtue is a positive quality and means behavior showing high moral standards. Virtues are the archetypes (essences) of God that we should acquire and develop in ourselves. Virtues are specific and acute lights that direct us to the Supreme Light who is God. The four cardinal virtues were recognized in classical antiquity and in traditional Christian theology. The term cardinal comes from the Latin "cardo," which means hinge. Some virtues are so called because they are the link or what is dependent for a virtuous life. The four cardinal virtues are prudence (wisdom), fortitude (courage), temperance (self-control), and justice (fairness). Justice is the most important cardinal virtue. The Ancient Greeks also used it to mean righteousness. These virtues were initially identified by Ancient Greek Philosopher Plato in his book *The Republic* IV

426–435 (Plato's *Protagoras* 330b also includes piety). Aristotle, too, examined them in *Nicomachean Ethics*. Roman Politician and Philosopher Cicero expanded on them, and Christian Saints Ambrose, Augustine, and Thomas Aquinas affirmed them and added the theological virtues ("Cardinal virtues," www.wikipedia.org. Accessed 5-10-2023).

    The three theological virtues are faith, hope, and love. And, love is considered the greatest of all virtues. They were first identified by Apostle Paul in 1 Corinthians 13. The theological virtues become a part of us because of God, not because of human will; while, the cardinal virtues come from human will. Both the cardinal and theological virtues become a part of the individual by means of practice. By exercising them, they will strengthen and increase in the individual ("Theological virtues," www.wikipedia.org. Accessed 5-10-2023).

    The opposite of virtue is vice, which is defined as immoral or wicked behavior. Vice is synonymous with sin - although the word sin is directly affiliated with the devil who is against God and has a religious connotation. A sin is anything that distances someone from God or comes between someone and God. Sins result in darkness of mind, darkness of heart, and darkness of soul. Sins can be classified into two categories: venial and mortal. Venial sins are relatively minor sins that do not result in eternal damnation of the soul by going to hell;

nonetheless, they cause injury to one's relationship with God. Mortal sins are grave sins that lead to separation from God and His saving grace. Without repentance and Confession to a priest, mortal sins can lead to damnation in hell. Ernest repentance and Confession can save the individual.

There are seven deadly sins, which are also known as the capital vices or cardinal sins. They are pride, greed, lust, envy, gluttony, wrath, and sloth. Pride is considered the most severe and is the sin that brought down Lucifer and made him the Devil. These sins are abuses or excesses of one's natural faculties. They lead to immoral behavior. They are not necessarily mortal sins, but they can become mortal sins.

As I said, this method of strengthening virtue and eliminating sin in myself was my initial instinct when I was 22 years old as I was looking for a path to God - and this method has Christian support. Dionysius the Areopagite's 5th century AD Christian masterpiece *The Celestial Hierarchy* prescribes a similar method, the angelic method to theosis. The masterpiece identifies God's most defining archetypes (essences) through the nine different Celestial Beings - commonly referred to as Angels. The masterpiece explains:

> The aim of Hierarchy is the greatest possible assimilation to and union with God, and by taking Him as leader in all holy

wisdom, to become like Him, so far as is permitted, by contemplating intently His most Divine Beauty. Also it moulds and perfects its participants in the holy image of God like bright and spotless mirrors which receive the Ray of the Supreme Deity — which is the Source of Light.

(III, Christian Classics Ethereal Library)

In Greek Orthodox Christianity, this holy God-like condition is known as theosis. To attain assimilation to and union with God - which is theosis - the masterpiece prescribes that we follow the lead of the angels and embody God's archetypes, like the angelic Seraphim who embody God's Agape Love, like the angelic Cherubim who embody God's Wisdom, like the angelic Thrones who embody God's Justice. Supreme is agape love. God is Agape Love. And, love unites us with God and each other. By embodying God's archetypes, like the angels, we will be purified, live more holy lives, attain union with God, and be more like God - which will lead us to greater happiness in this life and to eternal happiness in the afterlife.

For more on *The Celestial Hierarchy* and the angelic method to theosis, please read the exposition I wrote on the topic which can be found in my book *Beholding Heavenly Light: Lessons from Christian Masterpieces*.

God is the Source of all that is good, and we must become good like the Source to be gifted with blessings. Imitation of God's positive divine attributes is our return to divine likeness, yet this likeness is still far from the Source. God is Perfect Virtue, and we must participate in virtue to be with God. We never reach perfection of virtue, but we must, nonetheless, advance out to the Limitlessness that is God. Gregory Palamas taught that we can participate in God's attributes or energies but not His nature or essence, which is infinitely beyond our reach (Russell, 304).

The virtuous life is the return to our "natural beauty" and divine nature (Russell, 209). We must share in the divine qualities to attain theosis. As Russell explains when investigating the theology of Gregory of Nyssa, "a human being may 'become a god' through the imitation of the characteristics of the divine nature" (Russell, 226). We must free ourselves from evil and develop good qualities, such as humility like Christ, contrary to bad qualities, such as pride like Satan.

Desire for virtue is a spiritual desire, and forming virtuous habits will lead to benefits with heavenly rewards. Virtue nourishes the soul and is attained through progress and spiritual advancement. The aim is to attain likeness to God as much as humanly possible. Virtue helps to return and restore human beings to a godly likeness, and it guides human beings to a proper active relationship with

God. Neglecting virtue and falling with sin makes human beings into beasts instead of gods. We must participate in God's divine attributes for theosis.

The gods are those who reproduce within themselves the attributes of Almighty God. We must also imitate Christ - His attributes and life - to return to the divine likeness, which we lost. We must follow the example of Apostle Paul who declared in Galatians 2:20b (RSV), "it is no longer I who live, but Christ who lives in me." Christ is the preeminent example of virtue and moral excellence that we must imitate. The gods of theosis are all the saints who follow Christ. We must become Christ-like. By imitating Christ, we can restore our likeness to God and reciprocate our love back to God the Father and God the Son. By imitating Christ and His divine attributes, the faithful Christian shares in Christ's own nature and takes on a new identity in this life with an increased moral excellence and in the afterlife with a blessed eternal existence.

According to Clement of Alexandria, when a person studies and strives to attain the highest possible degree of glory and to become a god in high heaven, the person must perform perfect actions - which require intelligence, knowledge, good conscience, and divine grace - to be successful. Still further, the person must preserve holiness, be just, be pure in soul, be serious in thought, regard ignorance as evil, use right reason, and always thank God with righteous hearing, divine reading, true inquiry, holy sacrifice, and blessed prayer (which includes praise, hymns, blessings, and psalms). This is moral perfection, Christian worship, and Christian praise. Clement believed such a soul is always one with God. Such a soul loves God and serves God with constant close attention to his own soul (Russell, 132).

    Love is the preeminent virtue. There are four terms, in the Greek language, for the four forms of love; however, I am not referring to storge (familial love), philia (friendship love), or eros (romantic love). The love I am referring to is Christian love, the love that Jesus embodied, which is agape (selfless self-sacrificial love). Clement believed knowledge perfects a man as a man, but love perfects a man as a god (Russell, 133). We must imitate God's love for humanity and respond to God who loved us first. We must respond to God's divine philanthropy - His love for humankind - as expressed in John 3:16, which explains the degree to which God loves us and how we must respond to be blessed with eternal life. We must also imitate Christ's love for God the Father and humankind as exemplified by His life, teachings, and death. We must imitate Christ's extraordinary love, as expressed in His suffering Passion and death, by loving us more than Himself, by taking our condemnation upon Himself.

    In the Gospel According to Mark 12 (RSV), there is a lesson on the first and greatest commandment. From Mark, we learn:

28 And one of the scribes came up and heard them disputing with one another, and seeing that he answered them well, asked him, "Which commandment is the first of all?" 29 Jesus answered, "The first is, 'Hear, O Israel: The Lord our God, the Lord is one; 30 and you shall love the Lord your God with all your heart, and with all your soul, and with all your mind, and with all your strength.' 31 The second is this, 'You shall love your neighbor as yourself.' There is no other commandment greater than these." 32 And the scribe said to him, "You are right, Teacher; you have truly said that he is one, and there is no other but he; 33 and to love him with all the heart, and with all the understanding, and with all the strength, and to love one's neighbor as oneself, is much more than all whole burnt offerings and sacrifices." 34 And when Jesus saw that he answered wisely, he said to him, "You are not far from the kingdom of God." And after that no one dared to ask him any question.

Love is the preeminent virtue and is the foundation for the greatest commandments. Jesus embodied love and taught us to practice love. In the Gospel According to John 14 (RSV), Jesus explains how we should respond to His love:

15 "If you love me, you will keep my commandments. 16 And I will pray the Father, and he will give you another Counselor, to be with you for ever, 17 even the Spirit of truth, whom the world cannot receive, because it neither sees him nor knows him; you know him, for he dwells with you, and will be in you.
18 "I will not leave you desolate; I will come to you. 19 Yet a little while, and the world will see me no more, but you will see me; because I live, you will live also. 20 In that day you will know that I am in my Father, and you in me, and I in you. 21 He who has my commandments and keeps them, he it is who loves me; and he who loves me will be loved by my Father, and I will love him and manifest myself to him." 22 Judas (not Iscariot) said to him, "Lord, how is it that you will manifest yourself to us, and not to the world?" 23 Jesus answered him, "If a man loves me, he will keep my word, and my Father will love him, and we will come to him and make our home with him. 24 He who does not love me does not keep my words; and the word which you hear is not mine but the Father's who sent me.
25 "These things I have spoken to you, while I am still with you. 26 But the Counselor, the

Holy Spirit, whom the Father will send in my name, he will teach you all things, and bring to your remembrance all that I have said to you. 27 Peace I leave with you; my peace I give to you; not as the world gives do I give to you. Let not your hearts be troubled, neither let them be afraid. 28 You heard me say to you, 'I go away, and I will come to you.' If you loved me, you would have rejoiced, because I go to the Father; for the Father is greater than I. 29 And now I have told you before it takes place, so that when it does take place, you may believe. 30 I will no longer talk much with you, for the ruler of this world is coming. He has no power over me; 31 but I do as the Father has commanded me, so that the world may know that I love the Father. Rise, let us go hence.

Elaborating on a beautiful Old Testament metaphor about Israel as God's Vineyard (Isaiah 5:1-7) and Israel as God's Vine (Psalm 80:8-19), Jesus applies the metaphor's symbolic poetry to Himself and calls Himself the True Vine (John 15:1-17). Then, with literal language, He goes on to explain agape love and how He expects us to respond to His love. In the Gospel According to John 15 (RSV), Jesus says:

9 As the Father has loved me, so have I loved you; abide in my love. 10 If you keep my commandments, you will abide in my love, just as I have kept my Father's commandments and abide in his love. 11 These things I have spoken to you, that my joy may be in you, and that your joy may be full. 12 "This is my commandment, that you love one another as I have loved you. 13 Greater love has no man than this, that a man lay down his life for his friends. 14 You are my friends if you do what I command you. 15 No longer do I call you servants,[a] for the servant[b] does not know what his master is doing; but I have called you friends, for all that I have heard from my Father I have made known to you. 16 You did not choose me, but I chose you and appointed you that you should go and bear fruit and that your fruit should abide; so that whatever you ask the Father in my name, he may give it to you. 17 This I command you, to love one another.

In 1 John 3:16 (RSV), agape love is defined, and we learn about its altruistic nature. John explains:

> By this we know love [agape], that he [Jesus] laid down his life for us; and we ought to lay down our lives for the brethren.

Maximus the Confessor believed that as God became a man out of love for man, man can become a god with God through love (Russell, 278).

For more on agape love, please read my theological treatise "Agape into Eternity," which can be found in my book *In the Name of Salvation: Three Theological Treatises*.

(ii) Asceticism for God

Jesus and the Church teach us how to confront struggle for our benefit. The holy men of the Bible and the Church Fathers taught that the soul is meant to be purified by life's trials and tribulations in the same way that gold is refined by furnace fire. Although the soul is more valuable than gold, both are made better when purified and refined. The struggles in life can be harnessed to purify the soul. God allows these struggles for our benefit to purify our souls now in this life in this world, so we do not suffer in Eternity.

Asceticism is a self-inflicted struggle and is a wise way to purify one's soul. Asceticism is about self-discipline, which the Bible values as an important quality that a person should develop within oneself.

If you do not discipline yourself, then God - as Loving Heavenly Father - will discipline you, but you may not like the way He does it (Proverbs 3:11-12). So, it is wise to be self-disciplined and practice asceticism for God. Asceticism strengthens the soul and brings us to a higher spiritual level.

Asceticism is necessary to attain theosis. We should practice asceticism to eliminate our negative qualities and to strengthen our positive qualities. Asceticism can be defined as exercise or training for spiritual purification. This basic method of eliminating the negative and strengthening the positive within ourselves to reach union with God will lead us to greater happiness in this life and to eternal happiness in the afterlife.

The primary forms of Christian asceticism include prayer, fasting, and chastity without sexual lust. These ascetic practices prepare us for the Eucharist. Along with prayer, abstaining from certain foods (as prescribed by the Church) as well as abstaining from lustful sexual activity are necessary to receive the Eucharist. Alert prayerful activity, abstaining from foods, and abstaining from lustful sexual activity require self-discipline and are asceticism for God. With asceticism, we become spiritual athletes who are striving to win the eternal prize (1 Corinthians 9:24-27).

The struggle against the evils in life is remedied by the discipline of asceticism because asceticism trains a person in the best way to confront struggle and evil and in the best way to develop good habits for God - which will strengthen a person's relationship with God. It is important to understand that even for people who have excelled against evil, the struggle remains, but it becomes a good struggle. No longer is the struggle against the vices, rather the struggle is to continue to carry one's own cross daily and grow in virtue (Luke 9:23-27).

Asceticism helps to separate us from the passions and to overcome the passions. The struggle against the passions prepares one for contemplation. Chastity brings immortality to the soul and enables the pure Christian to contemplate God. In the Gospel According to Matthew 5:27-30, Jesus objects to sexual lust equating it to the sin of adultery. Jesus abstained from sex, and all the Saints fought off sexual lust. As Russell points out, Tatian believed that people should not even indulge in marital intercourse as Adam and Eve did after the Fall bringing them close to the beasts (Russell, 103). The gods are those who have put to death the desires of the body and live in spirit with the Holy Spirit. They transcend their human nature and live a divine life. They are no longer slaves to desire.

We must rise above the bodily temptations of this world and ascend with holiness toward the heavenly realm through asceticism. We must strive to free ourselves from the material world. This is possible through a transformation of self and a transformation of our human condition. Orthodox

Christian Monastics are the Church's members who are the most vigorous ascetics.

Asceticism is the ethical approach to theosis. It is a process of moral progress in one's life to abide by God. Asceticism is exercise of the intellect, will, and spirit to live morally upright in relation to God, self, and neighbor. God became man by emptying His Glory, and for us to be like God, we must equally empty ourselves of the passions (Russell, 268). Asceticism is a method for progress in moral life away from sensual gratification. It is used to renounce the passions of the flesh and rise in spiritual life through chastity, fasting, and prayer. With the vigor of a spiritual warrior, a Christian must conquer the passions, anger, and desire to attain theosis. As Jesus said to His disciples, "Watch[f] and pray that you may not enter into temptation; the spirit indeed is willing, but the flesh is weak" (Matthew 26:41, RSV).

Asceticism is not a virtue in itself - although it has the ability to manifest virtuous qualities. Asceticism is a method and aid toward theosis, although it is never the cause for theosis, which is only gifted by God's grace to His adopted sons and daughters. A person who has attained theosis no longer has conflicting forces within him and is whole, complete, and one with God.

Even so, life is a struggle. We must live life one day at a time (Matthew 6:25-34) and carry our crosses daily (Luke 9:23-27). Although theosis is possible, Basil of Caesarea taught that we can fall from elevated divinity through negligence (Russell, 208). The struggle is real. The devil is relentless, and the struggle in this life does not end. We must be vigilant and continue to pray to God for protection from evil and the evil one as expressed in the Lord's Prayer (Matthew 6:5-15). As the Macarian writings teach, the struggle against the devil and evil continues through life - regardless of holiness or theosis - up to death. Before death, no one is able to completely rest in peace. Practical responsibilities and the struggle remain. No one in this life enjoys continued uninterrupted communion with God (Russell, 243-244).

The moral struggle continues, yet the Holy Spirit is operative with the Son in our moral life. Ascetical struggle remains necessary and is accompanied with help from the Father, Son, and Holy Spirit. God helps those who pray to Him. We must strive for perfection with an ethical life. From our fallen state, we must aim to recover the virtuous life and original proximity to God. It is about progressive growth and moral progress by exercising mature moral choices. It is a process in which the intellect, with the help of God, becomes progressively conformed to God.

For more on asceticism and how it leads to theosis, please read the exposition I wrote on Athanasius's *Life of Antony*, which can be found in my book *Beholding Heavenly Light: Lessons from Christian Masterpieces*.

(iii) Contemplation of God

To attain theosis, we must strive for perfection through contemplation and reach the highest level of contemplation, which is to pray unceasingly. The Church Fathers believed heavenly contemplation of God is essential for theosis.

God by nature is a rational Being, and we human beings are blessed as rational beings, as well. Made in the image of God, we are blessed with the gift of rationality. The preeminent and highest form of rational exercise is contemplation. The contemplative life is a philosophical and theological life.

We develop a philosophical and theological life through reading and studying because reading and studying stimulate contemplation. We must become students of God and His teachings - which is possible through reading and studying the Bible and the writings of the Saints. Before attaining theosis, one must learn about theosis, and this is possible through reading and studying about God and His teachings.

People who read and study philosophy are thoughtful people who practice contemplation because philosophy encourages us to think more deeply and to contemplate. The English word "philosophy" comes from the Greek word "philosophia," which is formed by uniting two words: philia (friendship love) and sophia (wisdom). So, from the Greek, we learn that philosophy means love of wisdom. That means a philosopher is a person who is a friend of wisdom and a person who loves wisdom.

The foundation of Western Philosophy began with the axiom "know thyself," which came from the Oracle of Delphi and which was further popularized by Socrates. I believe Socrates knew what was inside of people because he was keenly aware of himself, and to know oneself is to know what is inside others. To know thyself is to know what dwells inside the individual and to know the human condition. I believe that we are all the same - we are all human beings all living on the same planet. We all experience love and pain, and we can all relate to each other's joy and sorrow. To be sensitive to one's own feelings and the feelings of others gives one compassion. To know thyself is easier said than done. It could take a lifetime, but if one perseveres, one will notice treasures multiplying within (Angelidis, *Young Ezekiel*, 59-60).

Philosophy develops, grows, and matures by exercising natural reason. The entire philosophical enterprise has been built with natural reason, which is respected and honored in the Eastern and Western Churches as a valuable light in a dark world.

The Church Fathers, such as Clement of Alexandria, believed that only a Christian can be a true philosopher, only a Christian possesses the truth. Clement believed the Christian philosopher shares the knowledge of his predecessors to bring his hearers to Salvation signaling true reverence toward God (Russell, 132).

The English word "theology" comes from the Greek word "theologia," which is formed by uniting two words: Theos (God) and logia (utterance or saying; the related word "logos" means discourse or reasoning). So, from the Greek, we learn that theology means the discourse or reasoning of God.

Authentic Christian knowledge is not esoteric knowledge, but rather is knowledge accessible to everyone who reads and studies the Scriptures. It is not reserved for the intellectual or spiritual elite, but rather for all who study the Christian Bible (Russell, 103).

Contemplation of God and contemplation of the divine characteristics is the path to theosis. Like virtue, contemplation nourishes the soul. It is used to grow and progress in the intellectual life and to look up to God's indescribable and incomprehensible beauty (Russell, 213).

Clement maintained that a person who exercises reason - away from participating in pleasures of the flesh - has mastery over the passions, is free from desire, and partakes in the unity and autonomy of God. Most Christians do not reach this level, but those Christians who do have attained the highest rank of the saved (Russell, 134). Heavenly contemplation is away from the pleasures of the flesh and away from their deception and toward the reality of God. Contemplation of God helps a theologian withdraw from material and practical activities to be with God. It is an escape from material desires and is towards a life with theosis.

    In the philosophical and contemplative life, the soul ascends to God but never reaches Him because of the incompressible gap between He and us. It is important to understand that the state of contemplation itself is not the soul's goal; although, contemplation is an activity to reach union with God. The pure soul longs to be in the presence of God in His Agape Love. The pure soul strives beyond itself as it reaches out to the Infinity of God. Progress and advancement never cease since God is Infinite and beyond us. Vision of God is the final goal - an indescribable joy - that is only attained in Blessed Eternity.

    In the Gospel According to Luke, there is a story that is cherished by theologians and students of theology because it affirms their instinct that learning theology is good and that it is the good portion that Jesus wants for us. The story in Luke 10 (RSV) takes place when Jesus visits Martha and Mary:

> 38 Now as they went on their way, he entered a village; and a woman named Martha received him into her house. 39 And she had a sister called Mary, who sat at the Lord's feet and listened to his teaching. 40 But Martha was distracted with much serving; and she went to him and said, "Lord, do you not care that my sister has left me to serve alone? Tell her then to help me." 41 But the Lord answered her, "Martha, Martha, you are anxious and troubled about many things; 42 one thing is needful.[e] Mary has chosen the good portion, which shall not be taken away from her."

In this story, we learn from Jesus that Mary chose well to listen to, contemplate with, and learn from the Lord. We should not follow the example of "anxious and troubled" Martha because as the Lord said, "one thing is needful." We should rather imitate Mary. The Lord Himself said, "Mary has chosen the good portion." The Good Lord further encourages us by reassuring Mary that it "shall not be taken away from her." Listening to, learning about, and retaining the word of God - specifically, Jesus' teachings - is more important than any other business or activity. This is the good portion. If we want the best food, we should go to our Lord and Savior Jesus Christ - "the bread of life" - who nourishes and fills our spirits (John 6:22-

71). Jesus leads us to theosis and eternal life when we consume His teachings and participate in His life.

Spiritual knowledge leads a person to theosis, and true spiritual knowledge is knowledge from Christ. Spiritual knowledge and moral effort produce a good soul. The goal of the contemplative life is knowledge of God. We learn about God through studying the Bible (the Old and New Testament Scriptures). Therefore, studying the Bible - with its heavenly teachings - leads to theosis. By reading the Bible, God and His teachings will live in our hearts and minds leading us to theosis. The Bible teaches us truths about God. The Church Fathers put the Bible together, and the Church's Saints help us interpret the Bible and instill in us divine knowledge and wisdom. Church Tradition is necessary. Without the Church and the devotion of Her Saints - who are our guides - people are likely to stray from proper understanding about God.

Aristotle and the ancient Greek philosophers encouraged contemplation because they believed that the contemplative life will lead to happiness. Contemplation in the philosophical life was a precursor to prayer in the Christian life. Just as the ancient Greek philosophical heritage believes in the contemplative life, so does the Christian heritage believe in the contemplative life, which is preeminently expressed in prayer.

I explained in the previous section on asceticism that prayer is a part of asceticism. Prayer is a huge part of Christian life and the means to theosis. Prayer is so big that it extends into the contemplative aspect of theosis. Prayer is a type of asceticism, and it is also a type of contemplation.

Contemplation is an activity of the mind, and the highest level of mindful contemplation is prayer - and to pray unceasingly. In 1 Thessalonians 5 (RSV), Paul teaches us to: "16 Rejoice always, 17 pray constantly, 18 give thanks in all circumstances; for this is the will of God in Christ Jesus for you." This is the heavenly advice that led the author of *The Way of a Pilgrim* to discover and use the Jesus Prayer:

> Lord Jesus Christ, Son of God, have mercy on me, a sinner.

Praying the Jesus Prayer constantly, without ceasing in our minds is the highest level of contemplation because it is how we learn about ourselves and God. By praying to God with our thoughts, we discover who we are and who God is. By repeating the Jesus Prayer in our minds, we learn about our human condition. The prayer fosters self-reflection. "Know thyself," insists ancient Greek philosophy. Through the art of prayer, we learn how to speak to God with our thoughts and develop a relationship with Him, who, as Augustine of Hippo explained, is "the witness of conscience" (*The City of God*, 14.28).

The Jesus Prayer is used continuously by Orthodox Christian monks; however, as exemplified by the Pilgrim, the Jesus Prayer is not only for monks and is also for people living in the world. You do not need to leave the world to contemplate and pray, so you can attain happiness, but time alone does help a person in the process. Monks know this, and they use the Jesus Prayer to cultivate happiness and, more specifically, hesychia - which is the inward stillness, silence, rest, quiet within the soul. They wisely live with other monks of like mindedness in monastic communities or live independently as hermits to focus on cultivating hesychia. These monks are known as Hesychasts and they practice Hesychasm. The Orthodox Church encourages men and women of all walks of life to attain, cultivate, and maintain hesychia for the benefit of their souls; although, monastics make hesychia a top priority. The inward stillness, silence, rest, quiet of hesychia within the soul is the key to happiness in this world and is a fruit of theosis. The Orthodox Church views the inward stillness, silence, rest, quiet of hesychia within the soul as one of the highest goods in human life.

In *The Way of a Pilgrim*, the Pilgrim's example also shows us that possessions do not lead to happiness because the Pilgrim finds happiness with the Jesus Prayer as he walks the earth without possessions. The Pilgrim shows us that what we need for happiness is a strong relationship with God. How do we develop a strong relationship with God? A strong relationship with God is based on love, and we love God by following His commandments, which are found in the Bible. As Jesus said, "He who has my commandments and keeps them, he it is who loves me; and he who loves me will be loved by my Father, and I will love him and manifest myself to him" (John 14:21, RSV). Also, in 1 John 5:3 (RSV), it says, "For this is the love of God, that we keep his commandments." A strong relationship also needs honest and free communication, and we can communicate with God through prayer, such as with the Jesus Prayer.

For more on the Jesus Prayer in *The Way of a Pilgrim* and how it leads to holy life, theosis and hesychia, please read my exposition on the topic. The exposition can be found in my book *Beholding Heavenly Light: Lessons from Christian Masterpieces*.

(f) <u>Experiencing Theosis</u>

Athanasius taught that our bodies are able to attain theosis because God the Son Himself took on a body and renewed the human body. We share in the theosis of the body that God the Son put on, which had fallen, but, through Him, is now exalted. The Incarnate God took on our nature in order to save it. Because He lived, suffered, died, Resurrected and

Ascended, we are no longer on the path to death and are now on the path to eternal life (Russell, 171-172).

When discussing Cyril of Alexandria, Russell explains that people arise from non-existence to createdness and have the potential to advance from createdness to transcendence. If people choose the good and acquire virtue, they can participate in the divine and recover their lost likeness to God (Russell, 191-192). Russell explains, "Those who are called to sonship by adoption and grace have transcended the limitations of their human nature and, while still remaining creatures, have come to participate in the life of the Trinity itself" (Russell, 196). When a person experiences theosis, the person ascends to a mystical union with the Holy Trinity. Every Christian who has attained perfection is blessed with theosis and becomes a god. The perfected Christian is a god, but only the Creator is Almighty God.

Origen maintained that the gods in the Old and New Testaments are "the saints, the perfect, those who live in beatitude. Through participation in God they have ceased to be men; having ascended to the supreme God, they have been transformed from men into angels or gods" (Russell, 146).

Possessing divine power is possible by developing a relationship with God, by communion with God, by growing in intimacy with God, who is Holy Trinity - Father, Son, Holy Spirit. Still further, to become God-like, one must become Christ-like.

The essence of theosis is to be Christ-like. Only then will we be transformed by divine glory and grace. The faithful believer is transformed by Christ and the Holy Spirit from a fallen human being into a god free from the limitations of death.

With theosis, the soul is filled with light and is illuminated by God's ineffable beauty and glory. The soul becomes worthy as a throne for the dwelling of God (Russell, 245). The Divine Light of God in us helps us see and navigate through the darkness of this world. The person is illuminated by a divine light that transcends nature. The soul is filled with light and love, specifically God's Light and Love; and God's Light is Supreme, and His Love is Agape Love. The soul moves towards God, and it is filled no longer with love of self and is filled, rather, with the love of God.

Dionysius the Areopagite maintained that we return to God through purification, illumination, and perfection (Russell, 248). This will lead to the soul's ascent to God and lead to the goal of theosis. When a person becomes a god, the person retains personal identity, but no longer lives in a human way and rather lives in a divine way. The human body no longer serves itself and the passions, but rather is trained by its soul to serve God.

Gregory Palamas vigorously taught that there is a distinction between God's essence and God's energies. He supported Hesychasm, which is a life of prayer and withdrawal to participate in the uncreated energies of God (Russell, 304). God's essence is beyond us, but we can experience God in this life through His energies, His operations. This would result in experiencing visions of the divine light, like when Christ's disciples witnessed Christ's Divine Light during His Transfiguration upon the high mountain as revealed in the New Testament. God may be apophatically unknowable, but He reaches out to us intimately with His energies, His operations. He participates in our lives, and by this, we know Him. Hesychast monks seek out this divine relationship and experience. They do not claim to understand God, His nature or His unapproachable essence, but they know He and His energies are real. Gregory Palamas taught that the saints - as gods who are sons of God - participate with God, but "only in that aspect of God which is participable" (Russell, 308).

In the Orthodox Church, the hesychast doctrine of theosis is the noblest expression of spiritual life (Russell, 309). As I mentioned, hesychia is the inward stillness, silence, rest, quiet within the soul and is the true fruit of theosis in this life because it leads to joy. Hesychasm is true authentic fruitful life, and hesychia is the fruit the mystic saints long to acquire. Even so, the hesychia and ecstasy of experiencing God's light and energies in this life does not compare to the bliss of experiencing God's light and energies in the afterlife.

As Russell explains, through the years, some theologians have reasoned that the term theosis (becoming a god) is only a title, metaphor, or analogy. The teachings of Symeon the New Theologian and Gregory Palamas emphasize that this reasoning is inaccurate and that theosis is an experientially realistic way of participating in divinity (Russell, 15).

When I read the Gospels and the Acts of the Apostles in the New Testament, I read the events as not only theology, but also as history. When Jesus and the Apostles performed miracles, I take them as historical events. The Apostles experienced theosis in a very real sense. Jesus Himself explained God's miraculous powers can be channeled through the asceticism of faith, righteousness, prayer, and fasting. We learn this in the Gospel According to Matthew 17 (RSV) when Jesus cures a boy with a demon:

> 14 And when they came to the crowd, a man came up to him and kneeling before him said, 15 "Lord, have mercy on my son, for he is an epileptic and he suffers terribly; for often he falls into the fire, and often into the water. 16 And I brought him to your disciples, and they could not heal him." 17 And Jesus answered, "O faithless and perverse generation, how long am I to be with you? How long am I to bear with you? Bring him here to me." 18 And Jesus rebuked him, and the demon came out of him, and the boy was cured instantly. 19

> Then the disciples came to Jesus privately and said, "Why could we not cast it out?" 20 He said to them, "Because of your little faith. For truly, I say to you, if you have faith as a grain of mustard seed, you will say to this mountain, 'Move from here to there,' and it will move; and nothing will be impossible to you."[b] 21, "But this kind never comes out except by prayer and fasting."

As I mentioned, asceticism is instrumental to theosis. It is the will of God that we practice asceticism. Through asceticism, we can possess powers of theosis. It is possible to heal the sick and exorcize demons through ascetic theosis. In the Gospel According to John 14:12 (RSV), Jesus explains, "Truly, truly, I say to you, he who believes in me will also do the works that I do; and greater works than these will he do, because I go to the Father."

Theosis is experientially real. The designation god - as expressed in the Old and New Testament Scriptures - is not merely a title, metaphor, or analogy. It is possible to experience God-like power through the asceticism of faith, righteousness, prayer, and fasting. Although, to be clear, powers from theosis are not generated by the individual and are rather generated by God. Powers from theosis come from God and not the individual. Human beings are only vessels of which God uses to fulfill His miraculous deeds. When God the Holy Spirit is in us, we can perform miracles, but the Source of the miracles is not the human being. The Source of a saint's miraculous power is God. God's miraculous power is channeled through His saints. God is performing the miracle - not the saint. God is using the saint to fulfill His Divine Plan, and the saint becomes God-like as an instrument of God's Divine Will.

So, attaining theosis and becoming God-like is not about pride and ego because the saint is not responsible for and cannot take credit for his or her divinity. Theosis is truly about sincere humility and submission to God who uses the saint for His Divine Will.

Since God is the Cause for theosis, theosis is not within our ability to manifest. It is not in our potential to possess - nor can we earn it through good works. Certainly, we must take steps toward God to gain theosis, but theosis is always a gift from Almighty God by grace.

The experientially real nature of theosis is further affirmed by Christian masterpieces like Saint Augustine's *The City of God* and Saint Athanasius's *Life of Antony*. I know that theosis is experientially realistic because I have personally experienced theosis as a citizen in the spiritual heavenly City of God as Saint Augustine taught it to me in his masterpiece. In addition, I have experienced similar trials with and victories over demons like Saint

Antony experienced - as revealed in Saint Athanasius's masterpiece - that serve as evidence for the experientially realistic nature of theosis. My book *Beholding Heavenly Light: Lessons from Christian Masterpieces* contains four expositions on four masterpieces - including the two mentioned above - and it is the first document I authored where I highlight the Orthodox Christian doctrine of theosis. The book is strong and tight scholarship that I encourage my audience to read. I believe you will find value in it and learn about the experientially realistic nature of theosis.

Through our relationship with God, our human nature can be transformed into a divine nature, which is theosis. We can escape the shackles of corruption in this world by participating in Christ and His divine nature. Clement of Alexandria believed that when a person attains theosis and becomes a god, he resembles the angels with their dual service to God and man - with worship to God and with instruction in the knowledge of God to man. However, Clement believed, in this life, a person studies to be a god and becomes a god only in Blessed Eternity (Russell, 132-133). Russell notes, "Deification [theosis] is the final end of humankind, the fullness of mystical union with God, seen in terms of a participation in the divine and uncreated energies which can begin even in this life" (Russell, 4). We do not reach full and complete theosis until after the end of time in Eternity with the General Resurrection in the presence of God. Theosis begins in this life but only reaches fulfillment and completion in the afterlife with God.

According to the Macarian writings, the perfect Christian - like Apostle Paul - who has Christ living in him (Galatians 2:20) - is blessed with theosis in this life, yet the struggle against evil continues up to death. Even Saint Antony the Great - a mighty ascetic and the Father of All Monks - had to guard himself against evil spirits. As long as we are living in this world, we all are susceptible to evil creeping into our hearts and lives. A saint is a person who is pure in heart, and as our Lord and Savior Jesus Christ taught in the Sermon on the Mount with the Beatitudes, "Blessed are the pure in heart, for they shall see God. (Matthew 5:8, RSV).

The Macarian writings explain that there are degrees of perfection and that we can experience moments with God in this life, but uninterrupted communion with God must wait until after death in Blessed Eternity. When analyzing the Macarian writings, Russell explains that the saints enjoy mystical experiences with Christ the Lord that are progressive, never end, and continue "towards an ever-increasing perception of divine light" (Russell, 244). Russell suggests that the faithful Christian's theosis occurs in three stages: (1) even in this life, the soul may participate in divine glory with the Holy Spirit as the person becomes a child of God, though these experiences are only a fleeting foretaste of Blessed Eternity; (2) at the time of death, when the body is laid aside, the soul is resurrected, glorified, and clothed by the Holy Spirit; (3) at the end of time, the body will join the soul in heavenly glory and illumination, and the body will be given a divine nature in the General Resurrection when the faithful Christians are fully christs, gods, and children of God (Russell, 245).

The greatest blessing of theosis is Salvation - the saving of soul and body from hell and into God's Eternal Kingdom of Heaven. Theosis may begin in this life, but it is not complete until the afterlife in the General Resurrection. The Resurrection of Christ is a pledge and promise for the General Resurrection of faithful Christians. In God's Divine Plan, human beings were created to attain theosis. The end for faithful Christians is a blessed eternal life with theosis as Resurrected Saints in the presence of the Holy Angels, the Most Holy Virgin Mother Mary, and God the All Holy Trinity in God's Eternal Kingdom of Heaven. Through the Scriptures and the Church, we learn that theosis is the ultimate existence in the eternal afterlife when there will be "a new heaven and a new earth" (Revelation 21:1), yet theosis is still mysterious to the human mind and is understood completely only by God. As Russell notes, Augustine of Hippo believed that theosis - when God makes men gods - is beyond human explanation and is to be "understood in divine silence" (Russell, 332).

Life is a struggle, but we experience moments of stillness and joy within our souls when we are one with God that suggest that there is more to existence than our experiences in this life. Because of such moments within our souls, I know that the soul is beyond the body and that the struggle for faithful Christians in this life will be replaced by rest in peace in the afterlife where they remain in God's eternal memory. Faithful Christians can hope for a blessed eternal existence with theosis in the afterlife where God - with divine grace and love - gives uninterrupted peace and incomprehensible happiness as the ultimate gifts to His children.

========================

BIBLIOGRAPHY

========================

When citing and referencing the Bible, I used the Revised Standard Version (RSV).

Angelidis, James Thomas. *Beholding Heavenly Light: Lessons from Christian Masterpieces.* www.jtangelidis.com: James Thomas Angelidis, 2021.

_____. *In the Name of Salvation: Three Theological Treatises.* www.jtangelidis.com: James Thomas Angelidis, 2016; 2017.

_____. "In the Spirit of Truth: Identifying My Three Theological Treatises in Church Tradition," 2017; 2019. https://www.jtangelidis.com/apologetics.html. Accessed 5-10-2023.

_____. *Writings.* www.jtangelidis.com: James Thomas Angelidis, 2016; 2017.

_____. *Young Ezekiel: A Life of Loves.* www.jtangelidis.com: James Thomas Angelidis, 2016; 2017.

Anonymous. *The Way of a Pilgrim.*

> French, R.M. (translator). *The Way of a Pilgrim and The Pilgrim Continues His Way.* Internet: https://jbburnett.com/resources/french_way_of_a_pilgrim.pdf. Accessed 12-23-2020.

> Savin, Olga (translator). *The Way of a Pilgrim and The Pilgrim Continues His Way.* Boulder: Shambhala, 2001.

Antiochian Orthodox Christian Archdiocese of North America. *A Pocket Prayer Book for Orthodox Christians.* Englewood: Antiochian Orthodox Christian Archdiocese, 1956.

Aristotle. *Nicomachean Ethics* (trans. by Martin Ostwald). Englewood Cliffs: Prentice-Hall Inc, 1962.

Athanasius [Saint]. *Life of Antony.*

> Gregg, Robert C. (translator). *Athanasius – The Life of Antony and the Letter to Marcellinus*. Mahwah: Paulist Press, 1980.

> Schaff, Philip (editor). *Athanasius: Life of Antony*. Christian Classics Ethereal Library: https://www.ccel.org. Accessed 10-21-2020.

Augustine [Saint]. *The City of God* (ed. and trans. by Marcus Dods). Project Gutenberg: https://www.gutenberg.org. Accessed 6-15-2018.

Brianchaninov, Bishop Ignatius [Saint]. *On the Prayer of Jesus: The Classic Guide to the Practice of Unceasing Prayer Found in The Way of a Pilgrim.* Boston: New Seeds, 2005.

Dionysius the Areopagite. *The Celestial Hierarchy.* Christian Classics Ethereal Library: https://www.ccel.org. Accessed 11-23-2018.

Francis, James Allan (attribution). "One Solitary Life." Bartleby: https://www.bartleby.com/73/916.html. Accessed 1-27-2022.

Gombrich, E.H. *A Little History of the World.* New

Haven and London: Yale University Press, 2008.

Guarino, Thomas G. *The Unchanging Truth of God?: Crucial Philosophical Issues for Theology.* Washington: The Catholic University of America Press, 2022.

Hopko, Father Thomas. "Foreword." *The Way of a Pilgrim and The Pilgrim Continues His Way.* Boulder: Shambhala, 2001.

Irenaeus [Saint]. *Against Heresies: Book V.* Christian Classics Ethereal Library: https://www.ccel.org. Accessed 10-21-2020.

Joseph [Saint]. *Monastic Wisdom: The Letters of Elder Joseph the Hesychast.* Florence, Arizona: Saint Anthony's Greek Orthodox Monastery, 1998.

Mathewes, Charles. "Books That Matter: The City of God." *The Great Courses* DVD Course with Guidebook. Chantilly: The Teaching Company, 2016.

The Nicene Creed. Greek Orthodox Archdiocese of America: https://www.goarch.org/-/the-nicene-creed. Accessed 5-10-2023.

Palmer, G.E.H. Sherrard, Philip. Ware, Kallistos. "Introduction." *The Philokalia: The Complete Text (Vol. 1).* New York: Farrar, Straus and Giroux, 1983.

Plato. *The Republic of Plato* (trans. Allan Bloom). [Second Edition] Basic Books, 1991.

____. *The Collected Dialogues of Plato* (ed. Edith Hamilton and Huntington Cairns). Princeton: Princeton University Press, 1999.

Richardson, Cyril C (editor). *Early Christian Fathers – Selections from the Work Against Heresies by Irenaeus, Bishop of Lyons.* Christian Classics Ethereal Library: https://www.ccel.org. Accessed 10-21-2020.

Russell, Norman. *The Doctrine of Deification in the Greek Patristic Tradition.* New York: Oxford University Press, 2004.

Ware, Bishop Kallistos (Timothy). *The Orthodox Church: An Introduction to Eastern Christianity* [New Edition, Third]. Great Britain: Penguin Books, 2015.

_____. *The Orthodox Way* [Revised Edition]. Crestwood: St Vladimir's Seminary Press, 1995.

_____. "Foreword." *On the Prayer of Jesus: The Classic Guide to the Practice of Unceasing Prayer Found in The Way of a Pilgrim.* Boston: New Seeds, 2006.

www.ingramcontent.com/pod-product-compliance
Lightning Source LLC
Chambersburg PA
CBHW071300110426
42743CB00042B/1119